Mark W.T. Harvey
OCTOBER 18, 1997
ST. PAUL, MN (WHA)

The American History Series

SERIES EDITORS
John Hope Franklin, *Duke University*
A. S. Eisenstadt, *Brooklyn College*

W9-BAJ-934

Arthur S. Link

GENERAL EDITOR FOR HISTORY

Robert W. Cherny
SAN FRANCISCO STATE UNIVERSITY

American Politics in the Gilded Age

1868–1900

HARLAN DAVIDSON, INC.
WHEELING, ILLINOIS 60090-6000

Library of Congress Cataloging-in-Publication Data

Cherny, Robert W.
    American politics in the Gilded Age, 1868–1900 / Robert W. Cherny.
       p. cm. — (The American history series)
    Includes bibliographical references and index.

    ISBN 0-88295-933-6
    1. United States—Politics and government—1865–1900. I. Title.
II . Series: American history series (Wheeling, Ill.)
E661.C46   1997
320.973'09'034—dc21   96-49864
                                                    CIP

Manufactured in the United States of America
01 00 99 98 97 1 2 3 4 5 MG

FOREWORD

Every generation writes its own history for the reason that it sees the past in the foreshortened perspective of its own experience. This has surely been true of the writing of American history. The practical aim of our historiography is to give us a more informed sense of where we are going by helping us understand the road we took in getting where we are. As the nature and dimensions of American life are changing, so too are the themes of our historical writing. Today's scholars are hard at work reconsidering every major aspect of the nation's past: its politics, diplomacy, economy, society, recreation, mores and values, as well as status, ethnic, race, sexual, and family relations. The lists of series titles that appear on the inside covers of this book will show at once that our historians are ever broadening the range of their studies.

The aim of this series is to offer our readers a survey of what today's historians are saying about the central themes and aspects of the American past. To do this, we have invited to write for the series only scholars who have made notable contributions to the respective fields in which they are working. Drawing on primary and secondary materials, each volume presents a factual and narrative account of its particular subject, one that affords readers a basis for perceiving its larger dimensions and importance. Conscious that readers respond to the closeness and immediacy of a subject, each of our authors seeks to restore the past as an actual present, to revive it as a living reality. The individuals and groups who figure in the pages of our books appear as real people who once were looking for survival and fulfillment. Aware that historical subjects are often matters of controversy, our authors present their own findings and conclusions. Each volume closes with an extensive critical essay on the writings of the major authorities on its particular theme.

The books in this series are primarily designed for use in both basic and advanced courses in American history, on the undergraduate and graduate levels. Such a series has a particular value these days, when the format of American history courses is being altered to accommodate a greater diversity of reading materials. The series offers a number of distinct advantages. It extends the dimensions of regular course work. It makes clear that the study of our past is, more than the student might otherwise understand, at once complex, profound, and absorbing. It presents that past as a subject of continuing interest and fresh investigation.

For these reasons the series strongly invites an interest that far exceeds the walls of academe. The work of experts in their respective fields, it puts at the disposal of all readers the rich findings of historical inquiry, an invitation to join, in major fields of research, those who are pondering anew the central themes and aspects of our past.

And, going beyond the confines of the classroom, it reminds the general reader no less than the university student that in each successive generation of the ever-changing American adventure, from its very start until our own day, men and women and children were facing their daily problems and attempting, as we are now, to live their lives and to make their way.

John Hope Franklin
A. S. Eisenstadt

CONTENTS

ACKNOWLEDGMENTS

In some ways this book began thirty years ago, when, in my second year of graduate school, I was assigned as a research assistant to John A. Garraty, then completing *The New Commonwealth, 1877–1890*. My major task that year was to verify all the footnotes in his manuscript by checking them against the original sources. By the end of that year, I thought I knew a great deal about the Gilded Age, but I have continued to learn about it ever since. I must first thank John Garraty for introducing me to the period and encouraging my interest in it; I owe similar thanks to Richard Jensen, Robert Zemsky, and Frederick Luebke who, shortly thereafter, helped guide me to the study of the "new political history" of the Gilded Age.

This book draws upon three decades of reading and teaching, in which time I have incurred far too many debts to librarians and archivists to list, even were I able to remember them all by name. However, two institutions have been, and continue to be, so important to my research that they and their staffs require mention. My colleagues at Leonard Library at San Francisco State University have always been unfailingly generous of their time and energy; for this I shall always be grateful. I also count myself extremely fortunate to be within a short commute of Doe Library at the University of California, Berkeley, the competent staff of which almost always has helped me find the book or journal I needed. Recently, the wonders of the internet even permitted me to use the University of California online catalog to check citations from halfway around the world.

Thanks are certainly due to those who read my manuscript and made its publication possible. James V. Compton and William Issel, my colleagues at San Francisco State, accepted this task with their usual good humor, and they tendered excellent advice. The editors of the American History Series, A. S. Eisenstadt and John Hope Franklin, made many helpful suggestions for the first draft's improvement, and three anonymous readers provided me expert reviews that were thorough and thoughtful; they not only improved my work but also saved me from committing several errors to print. Maureen Hewitt, formerly at Harlan Davidson, Inc., was unfailingly patient, understanding, and encouraging throughout all of this project's unanticipated delays. Andrew J. Davidson read the manuscript thoroughly and made many important suggestions for improving it.

I long ago discovered that one never thoroughly understands a subject until one teaches it. My largest debt, therefore, is to the students at San Francisco State who have taken my course, "History of the United States, 1877–1916," and seminars on the politics of that era. They gave me repeated opportunities to organize my thinking about the politics of the Gilded Age, and many times they raised insightful questions that made me rethink my approach to this work and the conclusions I reached. These thanks I also extend to the students and faculty at Moscow State University, where I am spending the spring semester of 1996 as a Fulbright lecturer, presenting lectures on the politics of the Gilded Age and Progressive Era even as I prepare the final draft for this book.

Three women in my life deserve special thanks. Rebecca Marshall Cherny could not possibly have known when she recited her marriage vows how much of her husband's time she would end up sharing with archives and libraries, but she always has done so with the same good-natured acceptance that she extends to the piles of books that multiply all over the house. Our daughter Sarah has graduated from the child in braids who helped carry her father's books to the library to the woman who handles the family finances while her parents are out of the country and, at the same time, earns As in organic chemistry. Finally, I thank my mother, Lena Cherny, for her consistent support and interest in all my undertakings, as well as for her unfailing cheerfulness.

While all of these people have contributed in various ways to this book, none bear any responsibility for any of its errors—they are completely my own.

Robert W. Cherny
Moscow, Spring 1996

To Sarah Catherine Cherny

INTRODUCTION

Visiting Washington in 1869, young Henry Adams, the grandson and great grandson of presidents, was surprised to hear a member of the cabinet bellow: "You can't use tact with a Congressman! A Congressman is a hog! You must take a stick and hit him on the snout!" Though surprised at the outburst, Adams soon found himself in agreement. Senators, he decided, were worse—they were grotesque, extravagant, egotistical, even comic, and they were doing "permanent and terrible mischief" to the nation. "The most troublesome task" for any president, he declared, was "bringing the Senate back to decency."

Adams was not alone in disparaging the politicians of the late nineteenth century. James Bryce, an English scholar who studied American politics in the 1880s, spent one full chapter of *The American Commonwealth* (1888) explaining "why great men are not chosen president" and another chapter on "why the best men do not go into politics." The critical views of Adams, Bryce, and others among their contemporaries found reflection in the views of many twentieth-century historians who described the politics of the period as devoid of content or accomplishment, as a mere spectacle to divert voters from thinking about the real issues of the day.

By focusing too closely on dramatic scandals and on the foibles of prominent politicians, however, the work of some historians has tended to obscure other aspects of Gilded Age politics that proved to be of great and long-term significance. Recent historians, accordingly, have taken another look in an effort to understand the characteristics and important products of late nineteenth-century politics: its voting behavior; the relation between the popular will and the formation of public policy; the cause and effect of the federal political stalemate that lasted from the mid-1870s to the 1890s; the sources of political innovation at state and local levels; and the political changes wrought during the 1890s that ushered in important new forms of American politics.

Politics underwent such fundamental change at the end of the nineteenth century that today's campaign rhetoric and political procedures bear little resemblance to those of the 1870s or 1880s. This book, therefore, begins with a chapter on elections and voting, the role and significance of political parties—from the grassroots level to Washington—and the way in which the parties of the day defined themselves. With the first in mind, the second and third chapters concentrate on the unfolding of national politics, but with due attention to local and state events that especially influenced developments at the federal level. The second chapter looks at the partisan stalemate that lasted from the mid-1870s, when the Republicans lost their secure national majority, to the end of the 1880s, when they seemed on the verge of regaining it. The third chapter examines the politically volatile 1890s, which witnessed the rise of a significant third party, the dramatic transformation of the Democratic party, significant changes in voting behavior, and the Republicans' resurgence to what proved to be an extended dominance.

This book is not a thorough treatment of politics in the period. Rather, it intends to provide a basic framework for understanding the often intricate political developments of the age. Throughout, it seeks to emphasize the underlying changes in the nature of politics that had as much, and often more, long-term significance as the ability of either party to command a majority in a particular election. The focus throughout is on the nature and workings of parties, the political process, and domestic policy. The excellence of the treatment of the period's foreign policy in Robert Beisner's *From the Old Diplomacy to the New, 1865–1900*, a companion volume in this series, makes it unnecessary to devote space to that topic in the pages that follow. Similarly, the treatment of the Grant administration here has a limited consideration of Reconstruction, because that topic has been treated with such thoroughness by other historians, notably Eric Foner in *Reconstruction: America's Unfinished Revolution, 1863–1877*.

Historians often label the years from the end of the Civil War to the end of the nineteenth century as the Gilded Age, and this term itself needs some explanation. Though in general use among historians and fixed in the name of the professional society for specialists in that period (the Society for Historians of the Gilded Age and Progressive Era), the term "Gilded Age" is no longer current among large numbers of Americans, even among academics outside the field of history. The name comes from a novel conceived in 1872, when, over dinner, the families of Charles Dudley Warner and Samuel L. Clemens (a.k.a. Mark Twain) disputed the merits of current best-selling novels. Though neither man had written a novel before, they decided they could do better than the books then in vogue. They succeeded. Their book, *The Gilded Age: A Tale of Today*, satirized the business and politics of their day, and for years afterwards historians often applied the name of the novel to the last thirty years of the nineteenth century.

During those years, the nation's steel industry boomed. The mines of the West poured forth a rich lode of minerals. Rail lines finally connected the Atlantic to the Pacific, bridged major rivers, and greatly increased their carrying capacity through new technologies, thereby creating a true national transportation network. American cities were transformed by the advent of skyscrapers, new forms of mass transportation, and a huge influx of new residents, many of whom had come from overseas. Individual inventors and newly developed research laboratories devised technological wonders such as telephones, electric lights, electric streetcars, calculating machines, phonographs, cameras, and "moving-picture" devices. Entrepreneurs like John D. Rockefeller and Andrew Carnegie and financiers like J. P. Morgan captured public attention as they reorganized American business by creating huge corporations that dominated entire industries.

The burnished locomotives spewing smoke and steam, the scintillating life of the expanding cities, the cornucopia of bright new technological baubles, even the glittering palaces of the new industrial entrepreneurs—all came to typify "progress" for many Americans, providing the gleaming surface of the Gilded Age. Just below that golden surface, however, lay twelve-hour workdays in factories, the widespread use of child labor, and large-scale business dealings so ethically dubious as to earn some entrepreneurs the designation "robber baron." Discrimination based on race, ethnicity, and gender was omnipresent.

The explosive social and economic transformations of the late nineteenth century have long attracted the attention of historians, who have probed deeply beneath the gilded surface of the period to study its sometimes grim social and economic realities. Its politics, too, have attracted a good deal of attention. Perhaps the actions of Rutherford B. Hayes, Grover Cleveland, Benjamin Harrison, and the other presidents of the Gilded Age inevitably suffer in comparison to Abraham Lincoln's confrontation with secession and slavery, Theodore Roosevelt's brash assertion of presidential authority against the coal companies, or Woodrow Wilson's efforts to ban war. But the significance of Gilded Age politics lies less in the actions of presidents, and more in the actions of the many Americans whose political choices ultimately worked a transformation of politics as far-reaching as the social and economic changes of the era, a transformation that laid the essential foundation for twentieth-century politics.

CHAPTER ONE

The Domain and Power of Party

Politics in the late nineteenth century differed significantly from politics today. Although the period's major parties were the Democrats and the Republicans, some differences are so great that a present-day American, were she or he somehow transported back to the Gilded Age, might not understand how to go about such a basic political procedure as voting on election day. Some of the most striking differences result from the greatly diminished significance of political parties. From the 1830s through the 1890s, political parties dominated American political decision making to a greater extent than ever before or since. Parties firmly controlled virtually all access to public office, all aspects of elections, and all aspects of policy making.

Americans then understood that "politics" meant *party politics*, and that all meaningful political participation came through parties. The parties of the Gilded Age had similar organizations and purposes: they nominated candidates, tried to elect them to office, and attempted to make their successful candidates write their policy objectives into law. But given the commanding role of political parties, any understanding of the politics of the Gilded Age must begin with an analysis of the parties: what they were; how they worked; what they stood for; and their relation to individual Americans, the state, and, ultimately, to public policy.

Parties, Elections, and Patronage

During much of the nineteenth century, the process of choosing a party's candidates for office and determining its stance on current issues theoretically began among the party's voters. At the most basic level of governmental organization—a township, ward, or precinct, whether urban or rural—voters gathered in party caucuses, called primaries, meetings open to all who lived in a particular district who identified with that party.[1] Voters who attended the primaries chose their party's candidates for any elective offices in their township, ward, or precinct. They also chose delegates to represent them at party conventions held at the next highest level of government, be it county or city. Theoretically, then, any voter could participate in this exercise in grass-roots democracy.

However, widespread participation in the primaries was not typical, especially in urban areas, partly because few issues or candidates motivated a significant turnout, but mainly because members of the local party organization often found it advantageous to discourage a large attendance. A case in point is the experience of Abraham Ruef of San Francisco, who, in 1886, discovered that his district Republican organization met late in the evening on an upper floor of a run-down boardinghouse in a reputedly dangerous neighborhood near the docks. When he worked up his courage and entered the meeting room, he found only two men present, who promptly informed him that he had just missed a large gathering

---

1 In our own time, at the threshold of the twenty-first century, most nominees for office are chosen in direct primaries, i.e., elections in which voters who are registered with a party choose their party's candidates. There were no direct primaries in the nineteenth century; instead, all nominees were chosen in party conventions, and the term "primary" designated the gatherings at which voters chose convention delegates. In the latter part of the twentieth century, such gatherings are rather rare, and, where they do exist (as in Iowa), are usually referred to as caucuses.

that had elected the two of them as district officers. Obviously, there had been no large gathering, and the newly "elected" officers had chosen the time and location of the primary to discourage attendance.

Moisei Ostrogorski, a Russian who studied American politics at the turn of the century, published his findings in *Democracy and the Organization of Political Parties* (1902). In it he suggested that only 1 to 10 percent of the eligible voters normally took part in the primaries, an estimate probably too low for rural areas but reasonably accurate for most cities. He also provided this picture of a typical primary in session:

The lists of the candidates voted on are settled beforehand, and very often each elector as he comes into the room receives several ready printed. True, every citizen is entitled to propose candidates of his own, but he will get no support in the meeting; and then the delegates to be chosen are often so numerous that a previous understanding is absolutely necessary. The lists presented at the primary are generally prepared behind the scenes, where the politicians 'make up the slate,' as it is said in their slang. Provided with the slate, the presiding officers of the primary make the meeting adopt it by a series of movements regulated with the precision of a military parade.

While the military-like precision of the political machine pictured by Ostrogorski sometimes broke down, his description caught the reality of most urban primaries well enough, and it rang true for many rural ones too.

Members of the local party organizations were usually the most significant decision makers in the primaries that fell within their jurisdiction. Such organizations, labeled "rings" or "courthouse rings" by their opponents, usually included the leading party activists—members of the county committee and sometimes the editor of the party's leading newspaper in the county—and some city or county officials. James Bryce described the ring this way: "a small knot of persons who pull the wires for the whole city, controlling the primaries, selecting candidates, 'running' conventions, organizing elections, treating on behalf of the party in the city with leaders of the party in the State." A ring's opponents often referred to its leader as the "boss," and the term came into general usage to designate the leader of any strong and well-disciplined party organization. The boss and his ring led an organization usually called a "machine"—a network of political activists bound together by personal loyalty to the boss or the party organization and each committed to cultivating and mobilizing the voters in his own neighborhood. After the dramatic revelations against New York City's Tweed Ring in 1871, accusations that a ring controlled local politics became fixtures of many primaries and conventions.

At the city or county level, the boss rarely held public office. Neither John Kelly, leader of the Democratic party in New York City from the early 1870s until his death in 1886, nor Richard Croker, his successor, held elective office while serving as party leader. A state party boss, however, sometimes held significant office, often that of U.S. senator—for example, Roscoe Conkling of New York in the 1870s and Matthew Quay of Pennsylvania in the late 1880s and 1890s, both Republicans. At that time, winning election to the Senate meant first winning a majority of the votes of the state legislators, so serious candidates for the Senate cultivated party activists in *all* the legislative districts in which their party had a chance of winning. Senators who were members of the same party as the president also expected to have the chief voice within in their state in awarding federal patronage—that is, appointing federal employees. These two circumstances practically guaranteed that U.S. senators either led a statewide "machine" or had close ties to one.

Delegates chosen in the primaries gathered for the next round of decision making in conventions at city and county levels. Among other decisions, county conventions selected delegates to state conventions, which in turn chose delegates to national conventions. County conventions also chose delegates for nominating conventions for congressional districts and various state districts—for every jurisdiction, in fact, in which candidates sought elective office within a state. Once assembled, most conventions followed a similar pattern: the delegates listened to countless and seemingly unending speeches glorifying their party and vilifying the opposition; they chose candidates for elective offices at their level of government; if appropriate, they chose delegates to the convention at the next level; and they adopted a party platform, a written explanation of their stand on current issues and their promises regarding changes in policy.

In most states there were candidates to be nominated every year. At the time, most states elected a half-dozen or more statewide officers, usually to short terms. In Ohio, for example, every year the voters chose one state supreme court judge for a five-year term and one member of the Board of Public Works for a three-year term; every other year they chose a governor, lieutenant governor, secretary of state, treasurer, and attorney general; every third year they picked a school commissioner and clerk of the supreme court; and every fourth year they elected a state auditor. Ohio was not unusual. In most states, voters elected several state officials every year. In addition, voters elected members of the state legislature and federal House of Representatives every other year, and elected district court officers and county officials at frequent intervals. Urban residents also elected a long list of officials, typically for two-year terms.

At many state nominating conventions, the selection of the party's candidates for office sometimes proved highly divisive. In most states during the late nineteenth century, relatively few officeholders sought more than two or three terms, so relatively few conventions opened with a set of incumbents seeking renomination. Instead, a convention usually opened with several candidates seeking nearly every nomination, including some incumbents seeking renomination, with a few or none of the prospective candidates holding commitments from a majority of the delegates.

During the convention, much of the work of assembling the majorities needed to nominate candidates took place informally, in small groups on the floor of the convention, or in restaurants, saloons, or hotels near the convention hall. Party leaders, candidates' representatives, and convention delegates argued over the candidates, counted delegates who already had committed themselves to particular candidates, and negotiated for the support of uncommitted delegates. The delegates from the same county or district sometimes voted as a bloc and let their delegation chairman negotiate on their behalf. Sometimes negotiations stretched late into the night in rooms cluttered with whiskey bottles and thick with cigar smoke, as candidates and campaign managers bargained with their counterparts and with delegation leaders. Though often played up by reformers, the booze and cigar smoke of the "smoke-filled room" should not be overemphasized. The important element at these power-broking meetings was bargaining. Such bargaining regularly took the form of *logrolling*—for example, a county delegation who were committed to candidate X for attorney general might agree to support candidate Y for lieutenant governor in return for promises from Y's supporters to support X.[2] Decried as corrupt by the losers and, of course, by the opposition party, logrolling was, in fact, typical of most political decision making in both parties.

State party leaders took special interest in securing a ticket broadly reflective of the party's voters and able to draw some votes from the opposing party. Sometimes these party leaders came to a convention with their list of preferred candidates in hand, the convention itself merely providing an endorsement of their decisions. Other times, state party leaders acted as brokers among various local delegations and among the various candidates seeking nominations. For state party leaders, an ideally *balanced ticket* included candidates who could be presented as representative of major regions within the state, of major economic and professional groups, usually including at least one each from business and agriculture, and of major ethnic groups who supported the party. A Democratic state ticket outside the South, for example, invariably included candidates with a following in Irish and German

---

2 Logrolling was perhaps the most widespread method of reaching a majority in legislative bodies and party conventions throughout the nineteenth century. The term itself comes from lumberjacks' practice of riding logs as they floated downstream. Two lumberjacks could stand on a log and roll it in the water by running on it. They had to synchronize their strides, however, or both would be pitched into the stream. As applied to political decision making, logrolling means that two or more legislators agree to support the same measure, i.e., to synchronize their efforts, because they both receive some benefit from it. Tariff bills were classic examples of logrolling, involving protection for the leading products of the districts of all or most of the members of the majority party.

immigrant communities. Among Republicans, it was also customary that the head of the ticket be a Union veteran. The ideal head of the ticket, especially when the party faced serious competition, was a man of unquestioned integrity and ability who appealed strongly to the party's traditional voters and also had some potential for winning support from the other party's adherents.

After each party's convention chose its candidates, and prior to election day, the parties mounted their campaigns, which were planned and carried out by party committees. Because state legislatures chose U.S. senators, campaigns for legislative seats in years preceding a senatorial election often drew intense attention. This gave the legislative campaigns a national significance they would not otherwise have had, encouraged party voting (and large voter turnouts) in legislative campaigns, and sometimes even eclipsed the campaigns for statewide offices. During all election campaigns, local party organizers sought to identify all their supporters, usually by talking to as many potential voters as possible. Campaign workers, especially in closely competitive states or districts, often maintained elaborate files on individual voters. Such files usually listed a voter's past party preference and key demographic information, especially ethnicity and occupation. As local organizers reported to state headquarters on the results of their contacts, state committees developed forecasts that often proved amazingly accurate and that permitted them, as well, to target campaign efforts to areas and groups of voters most likely to produce a margin of victory.

For voters, nearly all news about politics and governmental affairs came through the filter of party. Nearly every newspaper identified itself with a political party, and, especially at campaign time, each party subsidized the newspapers that supported its cause. In addition to these political subsidies, newspapers affiliated with the winning party often secured concrete rewards for their partisanship in the form of government printing contracts. Editors were often significant party leaders who held membership on local or state party committees. Throughout the nineteenth century, few newspapers drew much distinction between news and editorial comment. Instead, headlines, news stories, and editorials alike heaped praise on their own party and flayed the opposition with a vituperation that sometimes became highly inventive. Most communities outside the South usually had at least two newspapers, published daily in major cities and weekly elsewhere, one affiliated with each of the major parties.

During the month or so before the election, candidates and party dignitaries undertook speaking tours on behalf of the ticket. Local party organizations sponsored many community activities— displays by marching clubs, barbecues, rallies, and torchlight parades. Speeches inevitably capped such events, often going on for hours, sometimes punctuated by campaign songs that glorified the party's candidates and disparaged the opposition. Party organizers intended such activities to whip up enthusiasm for the party and its candidates, reinforce the loyalty of the party's usual supporters, and attract first-time voters.

All the hype and activities reached their climax on election day, when each party worked to mobilize its supporters to vote. One historian, Richard Jensen, has drawn a military metaphor for this form of politics: "Elections were treated like battles in which the two main armies (parties) concentrated on fielding the maximum number of troops (voters) on the battlefield (polls) on election day." On election day, party workers labored over lists of the party faithful and made certain that all their supporters made the trip to the polls. At polling places, party workers distributed lists or "tickets" of their party's candidates, which typically had been printed by the party's newspaper. Voters accepted a party ticket, sometimes printed on paper of a distinctive color and almost always headed by a party symbol, and voted by depositing the ticket in a ballot box. In many places, the ballot box sat on a table placed before a building's open window or doorway, in full view of election officials seated inside. Voters queued up outside the building, then filed past the window or doorway to vote. Voting was open— all the campaign workers could see which party's ticket a voter accepted and deposited in the ballot box.

Such a system encouraged "straight" party voting, in which the voter approved all the party candidates. Voters found it difficult to "split a ticket," because they had to cross out the name printed on the party ticket and write in the name of another candidate. Sometimes individual candidates and their supporters made this task easier by distributing "pasters," small slips of paper imprinted with the candidate's name on one side and impregnated with glue on the other. Party organizers, on the other hand, tried to make ticket splitting difficult; for example, they had all the vacant space on the ticket filled with decorative curlicues and elaborate ornamentation, so there was no space in which to write a name. One such contrived party ticket in California was so long and narrow and so filled with tiny print that it earned the name "tapeworm ticket."

Most voters, however, seemed willing to vote a straight ticket without such manipulation. Many, if not most, contemporary voters probably would have agreed with the observation by Roscoe Conkling, "boss" of New York's Republicans, that "I do not know how to belong to a party a little." Studies of voting behavior have confirmed that party loyalties in the late nineteenth century stood at all-time high levels. Many Americans considered intense party loyalty a part of a man's masculinity. Most men wore their party label proudly and proclaimed it in public; some even brawled over party differences. From childhood onward, the political culture of the era encouraged such intense loyalties and aggressive partisanship among males.

Political campaigning in which parties vied in mobilizing the largest number of supporters produced all-time records for voter participation. Between 1840 and 1900, more than 70 percent of the eligible voters cast their ballots in most presidential elections. In the presidential elections of 1840, 1860, and 1876, the national turnout exceeded 80 percent. In some states, turnout rose even higher. In 1876, 94 percent voted in Ohio, 95 percent in Indiana, and 99 percent in Iowa.[3] Given the parties' strenuous efforts to maximize their totals and given sometimes casual methods for determining voter eligibility, in a few closely competitive districts the total vote sometimes exceeded the number of eligible voters.

---

3 For purposes of comparison, voter participation in presidential elections from 1972 through 1992 ranged between 50 and 55 percent.

Once the votes were counted and the winners announced, political activists turned their full attention to appointing their supporters to government jobs. In the nineteenth century, government positions not filled by elections were staffed through the patronage system—newly elected presidents, governors, mayors, and other officials appointed their political allies to all the positions under their supervision, ranging from members of the president's cabinet and heads of federal agencies to local postal workers, courthouse clerks, and city hall janitors. Typically the appointing official deferred to local or state party leaders for appointments to offices within their jurisdictions. Nearly everyone understood that appointment to a government job was the appropriate reward for working hard during a campaign and helping to get one's candidates elected. Those appointed to government jobs, in turn, were expected to contribute a percentage of their salary to the party that had given them their job, just as party committees assessed nearly all candidates a percentage of the salary of the office they sought. Assessments from officeholders and candidates, in fact, constituted a major source of financing for campaigns and other party activities. This use of patronage for party purposes was called the *spoils system*, after Senator William Marcy's admonition, in 1831, that "to the victor belongs the spoils." Critics of the system labeled its defenders *spoilsmen*.

Since there were always more party loyalists than patronage jobs, elected officials invariably faced the often unpleasant task of settling a great competition for appointments. In 1869, when Ulysses S. Grant took office as president, Congressman James A. Garfield grumbled that "the adult population of the United States" all seemed involved in "the rush for office," a spectacle he found "absolutely appalling." In the late 1880s, Secretary of the Interior Lucius Lamar complained that "I eat my breakfast and dinner and supper always in the company of some two or three eager and hungry applicants for office." The historian who explores the papers of late nineteenth-century political figures usually discovers that the largest files are those related to patronage, often far thicker than those having to do with public policy issues.

Applicants aggressively sought all available government jobs. Those most in demand, however, entailed the dispensation of patronage—not only in the form of appointments to office but also of the purchasing of supplies and issuing of government contracts. Thus, the printer who published government notices, the building contractor who put up a public building, and the person who sold supplies to state agencies were all almost certain to be loyal supporters of the party in power. This system invited corruption, and many eagerly accepted the invitation. Entrepreneurs seeking contracts sometimes bribed the official responsible for awarding the contract, and some appointments, also, were reputed to be for sale. Only the imagination of a spoilsman limited his opportunities for personal gain. In the 1890s, for example, a high official in the Post Office Department pressured local postmasters all over the country to buy clocks for their offices—more than they needed—from a political associate of his.

A few critics found a fundamental defect in the system, quite apart from its capacity for corruption. By concentrating so much on patronage, politicians seemed to ignore principles and issues, and politics itself seemed to turn solely on greed for government employment. George F. Hoar, a Republican congressman from Massachusetts, accused some of his colleagues in 1876:

I have heard in highest places the shameless doctrine avowed by men grown old in public office that the true way by which power should be gained in the Republic is to bribe the people with the offices created for their service, and the true end for which it [power] should be used when gained is the promotion of selfish ambition and the gratification of personal revenge.

George Plunkitt, a local leader of the Democratic party in New York City, and many others like him in both parties, defended the spoils system. "You can't keep an organization together without patronage," he declared. "Men ain't in politics for nothin'. They want to get somethin' out of it." Plunkitt described a reality familiar to all party leaders. To win, parties needed huge armies of loyal retainers to identify and turn out voters and to distribute party tickets at polling places. Thus, the New York state Republican organization counted more than 10,000 local activists, and the Republican organization in Pennsylvania had more than 20,000. To mobilize their troops, party leaders needed the rewards that only patronage could offer.

Parties, the State, and Public Policy

Henry James, the novelist, observed in 1879 that the United States had "no State, in the European sense of the word." The United States, after all, had no state-established church and no state role for the clergy. It had no hereditary noble class to monopolize the top levels of the military and diplomatic corps. It had, in fact, virtually no military—federal military personnel never exceeded 40,000 between 1874 and 1894, and it reached a low of 34,000 in 1877. In 1885 the secretary of the navy announced that the nation had "nothing which deserves to be called a navy." The diplomatic and consular corps consisted of party loyalists appointed to foreign posts as rewards for faithful party service. Most of them had little idea what was expected of them, and some proved embarrassingly inept at diplomacy. Throughout most of the Gilded Age, the United States lagged behind Britain, France, and Germany in creating such attributes of a modern national state as a professional military and a career civil service appointed on merit.

In 1889, Woodrow Wilson, then making his reputation as a young political science professor, published *The State: Elements of Historical and Practical Politics*, in which he defined the state as an "organized force" that possesses and wields "authority"—a definition not unlike that of many political scientists today. Nonetheless, as late as 1906, one English visitor declared that "the typical American has no 'sense of the state.'" Indeed, most Americans had no "sense of the state" in major part because they so rarely saw any federal presence in their lives, much less experienced federal authority. An important exception was the Post Office, for its personnel accounted for more than one-half of all civilian federal employees throughout the period. The next most significant federal agency for many Americans was the Pension Office, which disbursed benefits to Union veterans with service-connected disabilities and to the widows and orphans of those who had died as a result of Union army service. The Pension Office dispersed one-quarter of all the federal expenditures during the 1880s, and more than one-third of the total during the 1890s. Neither the Post Office nor the Pension Office, however, represented a true exercise of state authority.

There was, to be certain, a palpable and sometimes authoritative federal presence at some times and in some places. During the Civil War, the authority of the national government had directly touched the lives of nearly everyone living in the nation, and during Reconstruction the federal government had exercised great authority throughout most of the South. The victorious Republicans dismantled much of that strong and centralized state at the war's end, however, and federal authority had largely vanished from the South by the mid-1870s. In the West, throughout the Gilded Age, however, the federal government was chief landowner, the sole constitutional authority for dealings with American Indians, and the major agent promoting economic development.

The prominent federal role in promoting western economic development was part of a larger federal policy for the economy, devised in the early 1860s and extended through the next four decades. (A policy may be defined, for this purpose, as a set of governmental decisions, over a fairly long period of time, that commit federal resources to the realization of some purpose.) The men who created the Republican party in the 1850s had included a number, mostly former Whigs, who advocated a more prominent federal role in stimulating economic development. The election of 1860 and the subsequent withdrawal of southern members of Congress presented the Republicans with the opportunity to create a new federal economic policy, and they wasted no time in doing so.

First came a new tariff law, passed in 1861. Before 1860, the dominant Democrats had set tariff rates largely on the need to raise sufficient revenue to meet federal expenses, which were few, given the Democrats' commitment to minimal government. The Republicans set the new tariff rates, however, to protect American manufactured products from competition from foreign-made products by making the price of imported goods equal to or greater than that of American-made goods. This, in turn, was expected to encourage investment in manufacturing. Such a policy, Republicans never tired of explaining, served the wage earner by protecting jobs and permitting wage levels above those of other manufacturing nations. By stimulating the economy, Republicans argued, the protective tariff benefited the nation as a whole.

At the beginning of the Civil War, the federal government claimed more than a billion acres of land as federal property, the public domain, more than half the land area of the nation. The Republicans set out to use this land to encourage economic development in a variety of ways. They provided free land for farmers, a policy begun with the Homestead Act in 1862 and extended in subsequent amendments. Recognizing the key role of higher education in economic growth, the Land-Grant College Act, also passed in 1862, gave land to states to fund public universities, which were required to provide education in engineering and agriculture. In 1862, too, Congress began a series of subsidies to western railroads by granting land to encourage construction of the first railroad to the Pacific, a project much discussed in the 1850s but long stalled by sectional disputes over the route. The Republicans did not invent the protective tariff or the use of the public domain to encourage economic development. Some politicians had advocated both for decades. With the departure of the South from Congress, however, the Republicans faced an unprecedented opportunity to put those proposals into effect and they moved quickly to do so in 1861 and 1862.

The protective tariff and the dispersal of the public domain are *distributive* policies, as distinguished from *regulation* and *redistribution*, other potential types of governmental economic policies. *Distribution* entails the government dispensing a benefit that requires no particular taxing strategy to fund. For example, the protective tariff taxed imports at their point of entry, but no person was directly taxed to support the policy. The distribution of the public domain provides an even better example. It had been in the federal government's hands for decades, and no one was directly taxed to provide land grants to railroads, universities, or farmers. Indeed, Congress even designed the railroad land grants so that the federal government would not lose any income from land sales—Congress gave to the railroad half the land within ten miles on either side of the tracks and, at the same time, doubled the price of the land parcels on the other half, thereby entirely recouping the cost of the railroad land grant. State and local governments also practiced a form of distribution when they scattered new state institutions to various parts of the state, subsidized railroad construction, and improved the infrastructure by building roads and bridges. Within the political system, distributive measures could also function as a higher level of patronage by providing concrete demonstrations of the benefits of supporting the party that had delivered these benefits.

Though the protective tariff touched the lives of many Americans indirectly, and land policies more directly affected many westerners, most federal distributive policies were remote from most Americans. In fact, during most of the Gilded Age, except for Reconstruction and western economic development, the federal government remained largely invisible to most Americans. There were no direct federal taxes; the only federal taxes that most Americans noticed were the excise taxes on tobacco products and distilled alcoholic beverages. Given the limited range of federal activities and the income generated by the protective tariff, there was, in fact, little need for any other federal taxes. Until 1887, no federal agency regulated economic activities. After 1887, when the Interstate Commerce Commission tried to regulate some railroad rates, it met court challenges, and the Supreme Court stripped it of any significant regulatory power in 1896.

State governments were somewhat less remote. By the late nineteenth century, most state governments provided a similar set of basic institutions—a university, one or more normal schools (to train school teachers), a prison, a home for disabled or elderly Civil War veterans, schools for the deaf or the blind, and custodial care facilities for the "insane" and "feeble-minded," terms then in use. States also maintained a militia. Additionally, by the 1880s, many states had established commissions to oversee railroads and occasionally other business enterprises, but many of those state commissions were highly limited to begin with and most became moribund after an 1886 Supreme Court decision seriously limited the ability of states to regulate interstate railroads. Most state revenue came from property taxes, assessed and collected by county officials rather than state agencies. State laws also regulated many social and economic activities—from the granting of divorces to saloon licensing, from the chartering of corporations to livestock grazing rights. Enforcement and implementation of state laws nearly always rested with local officials.

Most state constitutions specified that the legislature should meet only in alternate years, and most strictly limited the length of the legislative session. State legislatures, thus, typically met for only two to four months out of every twenty-four. Bryce summarized what he understood as the attitude of many Americans about state legislatures in this way: "If it meets, it will pass bad laws. Let us therefore prevent it from meeting." Recent historians have sometimes reached different conclusions. One, Ballard Campbell, noted that state legislatures may have produced "short-term solutions to many long-term problems," but that this marked them as little different from most policy makers at most times and places in American history.

If federal authority was usually invisible and state governments often remote, local governments—counties, cities, rural townships, school districts—were more obvious. A state government legally created all local governments within its boundaries and had ultimate control over them, but few Americans thought much about such distinctions. Instead, most people looked to local government for nearly all governmental services. Local school boards managed the public schools (grades 1–8) and, toward the end of the Gilded Age in cities and towns, public high schools. As late as 1902, local schools constituted the largest single category of governmental expenses, accounting for 14 percent of combined federal, state, and local governmental expenditures. Local government built and maintained nearly all streets and roads. County officials assessed the value of property for taxes, which other county officials levied and collected. Property tax was the most prevalent form of taxation in Gilded Age America, comprising more than two-thirds of all state and local revenue as late as 1902. Local officials implemented and enforced most laws, and those who violated them found themselves before a local justice of the peace, county judge, or district court judge. The most hotly debated political issues were often local ones having to do with such things as roads, schools, saloon licenses, and property tax levies.

Nearly all of those who administered local government were elected to do so, typically for two-year terms. These officers included members of school boards, rural township boards, justices of the peace, city councils and city officials (mayor, attorney, auditor, and others), county boards and county officials (sheriff, clerk, treasurer, auditor, assessor, school superintendent, judge, attorney, coroner), and officers of the district court (judge, attorney, clerk). In small towns and rural areas, where the majority of Americans still lived, transactions with the government almost always meant dealings with local officials—members of the same community, perhaps even members of the same church or fraternal order.

These same local officials also made up an important part of the countenance that political parties presented to voters. Within large cities, machines bridged the many formal political decision-making arenas and provided the most reliable channel for anyone seeking to influence city hall. The chain of party conventions reaching from the precinct caucuses to the national nominating convention provided a real and important link between local concerns and national debates on issues such as the tariff or monetary policy. In the decentralized federal system, where the Constitution broke up power into tiny fragments and dispersed it among many agencies, party organizations provided the most important way to mediate disagreements, to centralize decision making, and to mobilize the authority of the state. Parties controlled access to nearly all elective and appointive governmental offices, coordinated legislative activities with those of the executive branch, and linked the layers of the federal system with each other. Parties formed not just the nerves and sinews of the body politic—they constituted, in fact, nearly all of the body politic.

The Major Parties: The Republicans and The Democrats

Political parties linked all the different levels of political activity in nineteenth-century America. At the local level of the federal system, parties mobilized voters on election day by stressing those issues which defined local party loyalties. At the state and national levels of the federal system, parties might emphasize quite different issues. Yet there was a central core to both major parties' political rhetoric that connected their stands on local, often ethnocultural, issues and their position on federal, often economic, policies.

Sometimes called the Grand Old Party (GOP) after 1880, the Republicans of the Gilded Age developed three themes repeatedly in their platforms, newspapers, speeches, and campaign appeals: patriotism, prosperity, and morality. Republicans pointed to their successful defense of the Union during the Civil War and claimed a virtual monopoly on *patriotism*. A generation of Republican campaigners maintained the tone set by Oliver P. Morton, an Indiana Republican, when in 1866 he claimed that "the Democratic party may be described as a common sewer and loathsome receptacle, into which is emptied every element of treason North and South." Republican campaign orators often "waved the bloody shirt," an expression that dated back to 1866, when a Republican in the House of Representatives displayed the blood-stained shirt of a northern Republican who had been beaten by southerners, probably Democrats, to underline his condemnation of white supremacist terrorism. "Waving the bloody shirt" came to symbolize accusations that Democrats in general, and southern Democrats in particular, had proven themselves disloyal during the Civil War and refused to accept defeat at the war's end. Robert Ingersoll was among the Republicans most accomplished at this form of rhetoric:

I want you to know that every man who thinks the State is greater than the Union is a Democrat. Every man that declared [for] slavery was a Democrat. Every man that signed an ordinance of secession was a Democrat. Every man that lowered our flag from the skies was a Democrat. . . . Every man that shot a Union soldier was a Democrat.

The Republicans never tired of proclaiming that, having saved the Union in war, they alone deserved to administer the Union in peace.
Beyond its appeal to Civil War loyalties, this rhetoric also emphasized that the Republicans had been willing to use the power of the federal government at a time when leading Democrats fretted over the constitutionality of such action or advocated that the South be permitted to withdraw from the Union in peace. Republican party leaders looked to the Civil War in other ways, too. At the prompting of Republicans, Congress provided generous federal pensions to disabled Union Army veterans and to the widows and orphans of those who had died.
Republican party leaders carefully cultivated members of the Grand Army of the Republic (or GAR, the organization of Union veterans), attended their meetings, and urged them to "vote as you shot." One poll of Civil War veterans in Indiana in 1880 found that 69 percent voted Republican and only 25 percent were Democrats, with the remainder committed to third parties. It is no coincidence that in eight of the nine presidential elections between 1868 and 1900, the Republican candidate was a Union veteran. The sole exception, James G. Blaine, lost in 1884. Similar patterns held true at the state and local level throughout the North. During the 1880s in Nebraska, for example, four out of five Republican leaders were Union veterans, compared to a very few of the leading Democrats.
A second persistent Republican campaign theme was *prosperity*. Republicans pointed to the economic growth of the postwar era and argued that it stemmed largely from policies they had initiated, especially their protective tariff, land distribution, and monetary policies. Compared to their Democratic predecessors, the Republicans had, in fact, substantially altered the role of the federal government in the economy by using federal power to encourage economic development.
The Republicans' third persistent campaign theme was respectability and *morality*. In 1888, for example, the Republican national

convention adopted a resolution sympathizing with "all wise and well-directed efforts for the promotion of temperance and morality"—an acknowledgment of the growing number of opponents of alcohol. Senator George Hoar, in 1889, spoke for many of his party when he argued that the respectable element in the nation "commonly, and as a rule, by the natural law of their being, find their place in the Republican party." He produced a long list of examples, including "the men who do the work of piety and charity in our churches," farmers who worked their own fields, skilled workers, and "the men who saved the country in war, and have made it worth living in in peace." At the same time, Republicans delighted in portraying Democrats as "the old slave-owner and slave-driver, the saloon-keeper, the ballot-box-stuffer, the Kuklux [Klan member], the criminal class of the great cities, the men who cannot read or write," and they usually threw in a mention of the Tweed Ring for good measure.

Contrary to such depictions, throughout much of the Gilded Age, Democrats based their platforms on principles initially developed by Samuel Tilden, a prosperous attorney who led the revival of the Democratic party in New York state during the early 1870s. Tilden prescribed a program of minimal government: opposition to the protective tariff (preferring "a tariff for revenue only"); honesty in office; minimal governmental expenditures and minimal taxation; opposition to governmental subsidies or privileges for particular groups; and a conservative monetary policy. True to such platform pronouncements, most Democrats in Congress opposed the protective tariff, arguing that it raised prices paid by consumers in order to protect manufacturers from international competition. Democratic platforms usually opposed land grants for corporations on the grounds that the public domain should be reserved to provide farms for citizens. All in all, Democrats' view of the proper federal role in the economy came much closer to laissez-faire than did the Republicans' practice, for most Democrats opposed what one leading Democrat called "governmental interference" in the economy.

Thus, where Republicans defined themselves in terms of what their party did and who they were, Democrats typically crafted their identity in terms of what they opposed. Their commitment to minimal government harked back to the days of Andrew Jackson, who equated governmental activism with official privileges for a favored few. [One Democratic state platform in 1880 defined the ideal state this way: "The prosperous commonwealth is that one which legislates the least as to the relations between labor and capital, which enacts the fewest laws of a regulatory character, most unfrequently invades the domain of political economy with statutes, and draws the least amount of annual taxes from its citizens."] Democrats also accused the Republicans of "extravagant appropriations and expenses."

Just as the Democrats opposed governmental interference in the economy, so too did they oppose governmental interference in social relations and behavior. In the North, especially in Irish and German communities, Democrats staunchly opposed prohibition and, usually, other efforts intended to limit access to alcohol, such as restricting the number of saloons by requiring expensive licenses, which they condemned as infringements on personal liberty. Democrats also defended Catholics against the political attacks of groups like the American Protective Association (APA), an anti-Catholic group born in Iowa in 1887 that swept across the Midwest and into some other parts of the country in the late 1880s and early 1890s. APA members swore never to vote for a Catholic and sought to remove Catholics from all elective and appointive governmental positions. Usually working within the Republican party, the APA won majorities on a number of midwestern city councils and school boards in the early 1890s and sometimes influenced Republican candidates for congressional or state office. Democrats condemned such religious discrimination and insisted on the Constitution's guarantee of no religious requirements for holding public office.

Race was another matter. Until the passage of the Fourteenth and Fifteenth amendments, Democrats everywhere had generally agreed, in the words of one midwestern state platform of 1868, that "the right of suffrage should be entrusted only to the white race, through which civilization and enlightenment have come to us, and in whose hands alone the welfare of this State should repose." After the new amendments extended citizenship to African Americans and voting rights to African-American males, the 1872 Democratic national platform acknowledged "the equality of all men before the law." However, they consistently opposed federal enforcement of the rights of African Americans. "Local self-government," the 1872 platform went on to say, "will guard the rights of all citizens more securely than any centralized power." Across the South, "local self-government" usually looked the other way as Democrats established control over local and state politics, sometimes through fraud, coercion, intimidation, violence, and even assassination. Southern Democrats left no doubt of their commitment to white supremacy and developed their own counterpart to "waving the bloody shirt" as they merged their support for white supremacy with an emotional appeal to the "Lost Cause" of the Confederacy.

Democrats outside the South generally accepted and usually defended white supremacy. Throughout the West, companies consistently paid Chinese immigrants less than other workers. There, Democrats often took the lead in denouncing the Chinese for undercutting wages and called for an end to Chinese immigration. In 1882, when the Senate voted on a proposal to deny citizenship to Chinese immigrants already living in the United States, Democrats were unanimously in favor, but Republicans voted five to one against. Similarly, a few years before, most Democrats had opposed and most Republicans had favored a bill extending citizenship to American Indians. Thus, though Democrats generally proved more tolerant of religious diversity than Republicans, they often showed themselves less tolerant of racial differences.

All in all, Republicans presented themselves as believing in an active government, the one that had acted to save the Union, abolish slavery, stimulate economic development, and promote a more virtuous society. Democrats denounced the Republicans' activism as they argued for minimal government, personal liberty, white supremacy, and states' rights. As Thomas Reed, Republican Speaker of the House of Representatives in the early 1890s, put it, "The Republican party does things, the Democratic party criticizes." Neither party advocated government action to regulate, restrict, or tax the newly developing industrial corporations.

The significant differences in the parties' positions on issues were a reflection of the important differences between Republican and Democratic voters. Among the historians who have analyzed voting behavior, Paul Kleppner stands out for the depth, breadth, and number of his studies. He concluded that, during the Gilded Age, northern Catholics voted Democratic by margins of 70-30 or more, with the strongest Democratic loyalties among Irish Catholics. Those of German ancestry, regardless of religion, also tended to vote Democratic. Throughout the North and much of the West, the attitude of ethnocultural groups toward prohibition often provided the most accurate barometer of their party orientation: the more strongly a group opposed prohibition, the more likely they were to vote Democratic. This is not to say that one caused the other, only that the two were closely associated.

In the South, where the Democrats presented themselves as the party of white supremacy, they secured the votes of most white voters. In the eyes of southern Democrats, Republicans were the Yankees who had devastated their homeland and imposed Reconstruction upon them. Strong social pressures existed for southern whites to support the Democrats. Transplanted white southerners and their descendants in the lower Midwest and the West typically voted Democratic too.

After the collapse of the last of the Reconstruction-era Republican administrations in the southern states shortly after the 1876 elections, the Democrats dominated the southern and usually the border states, although the expression "Solid South" is better reserved for the period after the 1890s. Democrats also attracted enough northern voters to make them highly competitive in several states in that region. The Democrats, however, composed a very heterogeneous coalition, one held together primarily because its various components often could unite *against* governmental involvement in social relations or the economy.

The Republicans held regional bases in New England, upstate New York, Pennsylvania, and the upper Midwest. As with northern Democrats, ethnicity and religion provide the most reliable indicators of Republican-party affiliation. Old-stock New Englanders—those whose families had lived in the United States for several generations—and their descendants across the middle Atlantic and midwestern states were among the strongest Republicans. Kleppner found that, among old-stock northerners, 75 percent of Methodists and Congregationalists voted Republican, as did 65 percent of Baptists, and 60 percent of Presbyterians. Among immigrant groups, 80 percent of Swedish and Norwegian Lutherans voted Republican, as did two-thirds of British Protestants. African Americans, North and South, strongly supported the Republicans as the party of emancipation. So did most veterans of the abolition movement. Unlike their coreligionists elsewhere, Catholics of Mexican descent in New Mexico Territory and California divided more evenly between Republicans and Democrats, due largely to complicated state and territorial political maneuvering; most of the prominent, land-owning *mexicano* families, however, aligned with the Republicans.

Thus, outside the South, ethnicity and religion prove the most reliable predictors of party affiliation. Members of those religious groups identified by historians as *evangelical, pietist,* or *perfectionist*—Methodist, Baptist, Congregational, Presbyterian, Swedish and Norwegian Lutheran—defined sin broadly. The following list of sinful behavior appeared in *The Doctrines and Discipline of the Methodist Episcopal Church* in 1896:

indulging [in] sinful tempers or words, the buying, selling, or using intoxicating liquors as a beverage, signing petitions in favor of granting license for the sale of intoxicating liquors, becoming bondsmen for persons engaged in such traffic, renting property as a place in or on which to manufacture or sell intoxicating liquors, dancing, playing at games of chance, attending theaters, horse races, circuses, dancing parties, or patronizing dancing schools, or taking such other amusements as are obviously of misleading or questionable moral tendency.

Members of the pietist groups felt an obligation not only to perfect their own lives by eschewing all sinful behavior, but also to perfect their society as well. Outside the South, most members of these religious groups voted Republican, for the party of active government and morality.

By contrast, members of those groups variously identified as *liturgical* or *confessional*—Catholics, most German Lutherans, many Episcopalians—defined sin more narrowly. They saw no harm in the moderate consumption of alcoholic beverages, held dances in church halls, and conducted lotteries—which pietists condemned as "games of chance"—to raise money for their churches. Members of confessional groups typically voted Democratic, for the party of personal liberty that opposed using government to enforce any group's definition of proper behavior.

Most northern voters thus affiliated with the party that most closely corresponded to their ethnoreligious identity, and most southerners chose a party based on racial considerations. In comparison with ethnicity and race, the protective tariff seems to have exercised relatively little influence on the partisan choices of most voters, despite all the attention that it received in politics in the Gilded Age. To be certain, when a tariff bill was before Congress, it received extensive coverage in the newspapers. Those who debated the tariff on the floor of Congress or who harangued gatherings of the party faithful on the tariff during election campaigns were greeted with great enthusiasm. But many manufacturers and other business leaders, who usually supported both the protective tariff and its Republican sponsors, also tended to be old-stock Protestants from New England and the Northeast. Those entrepreneurs who believed that the protective tariff stifled international competition, and who thereby supported the Democratic critics of protection, included many southerners involved in the export of cotton and tobacco. With the exception of a handful of ideological free traders and perhaps a somewhat larger number of protectionists, few Americans seem to have made partisan choices based on the tariff. Edward Stanwood, after compiling an exhaustive history of the tariff published in 1903, claimed to have found "no evidence of any sort" that ordinary voters "were thinking about the tariff."

Nor, it seems, did many Americans vote their pocketbooks in other ways, at least in campaigns for national offices. Poor and working-class voters in the big cities typically supported the local machine, whether Democratic or Republican, but more big-city organizations were Democratic than were Republican. Many of the poor and working-class supporters of the big-city Democratic organizations came from the ethnic groups who voted

Democratic anyway. Organizations that claimed to speak for labor during much of the Gilded Age—the National Labor Union in the 1870s, the Knights of Labor in the 1880s, and the American Federation of Labor (AFL) after 1886—usually did not endorse presidential candidates, although local labor organizations and leaders sometimes made endorsements. Republicans and Democrats both pledged their friendship for labor. For the most part, the urban working class, like the poor, the urban middle class, and farmers, tended to divide politically along ethnic, religious, and racial lines rather than by class or occupation. Still, Kleppner found that as many as 25 to 40 percent of northern voters did not share the partisan commitments of their coreligionists. For some of them, partisan identities may have been linked less to ethnicity and more to their economic status.

Among historians who have recently studied workers' behavior at specific job sites or in specific communities, many have found that some workers developed an identification with other workers as an economic class, that significant numbers of them sometimes acted on the basis of such a class consciousness, and that such actions sometimes took on political dimensions. Terence V. Powderly, leader of the Knights of Labor and the nominee of a labor party, won election as mayor of Scranton, Pennsylvania, in 1878, 1880, and 1882. The Workingmen's Party of California, combining class appeals with the scapegoating of Chinese immigrants, elected one-third of the delegates to a state constitutional convention in 1878 and carried the San Francisco mayoralty election of 1879. In 1886, labor parties captured nearly one-third of the vote in New York City and more than one-quarter of the vote in Chicago. (Labor parties are discussed at more length later in this chapter.)

Few have attempted to reconcile the findings of the historians who have emphasized the ethnocultural basis of northern politics with the findings of those who have depicted the extent of class consciousness and class animosity. Significantly, most labor parties were local and short lived. Efforts to mobilize support for *national* labor parties proved dismal failures. Thus, it would seem that voters found it possible to cast a vote for a local labor party without altering their long-term commitment to one of the major national parties. Indeed, sometimes the Democrats or Republicans allied themselves with a local labor party, supporting it locally in return for its commitment of support in state and national elections. Furthermore, the voting system itself discouraged the growth of national third parties because success in a national election required that a party have an organizational presence at every polling place in the country.

Thus, although *some* voters in *some* areas at *some* times had a strong sense of class identity, *most* voters *most* of the time responded to one of the two major parties in terms of ethnicity, religion, and race. All in all, the Republicans represented a more homogeneous coalition—largely Protestant, largely in agreement on moral values, and committed to a positive view of government to accomplish limited social and economic goals. Democrats showed more religious heterogeneity, for the two largest blocs of Democrats consisted of northern Catholics and southern white old-stock Protestants; these groups differed fundamentally in their definitions of proper personal behavior, i.e. sin, but their political alliance was cemented by their common opposition to the strong use of government. Within local communities, intense party loyalties drew strength from the convergence of ethnicity, religion, race, and party, and from the absence, at most times and in most places, of significant cross-cutting allegiances derived from economic factors.

On the Periphery of Party Politics:
Mugwumps, Suffragists, Prohibitionists, Grangers, Greenbackers, and Laborites

Despite the power of the major parties and the high degree of party loyalty among most voters, a few Americans challenged the basic features of the political system. Quite different, although occasionally overlapping, groups organized to seek measures that the major parties rarely addressed: abolition of the spoils system; woman suffrage; prohibition; regulation of railroad rates; changes in federal monetary policy; and institution of the secret ballot.

One group, whom some historians have called "genteel reformers," largely fit James Bryce's description: "a section of the Republican party, more important by the intelligence and social position of the men who composed it than by its numbers." Centered in Boston and New York City, many of these reform-minded Republicans came from prominent old-stock families, had graduated from prestigious colleges, and held high social status. During the 1884 election, their critics labeled them Mugwumps, and historians have often applied that name retrospectively as well. At the time, some claimed that the name derived from an Indian word for a young man who thought he knew better than his elders. Another version described the mugwump as a bird sitting on a fence, with its "mug" on one side and its "wump" on the other. To be called a fence-sitter was also an insult, applied to those unable to make up their minds, such as this group of Republicans who sometimes seemed uncertain about supporting their party's candidates. The Mugwumps themselves redefined the word to mean a person who acted on principle rather than blind party loyalty.

Most Mugwumps championed laissez-faire economics, but the spoils system aroused them to indignation. Tracing many of the evils they saw in politics to the operation of patronage, they argued that eliminating patronage would drive the machines, rings, and bosses out of politics and thereby restore political purity and decency. As an alternative to the spoils system, they proposed a civil service based on merit, with appointments going to those who scored highest on an examination. Great Britain had implemented such a merit system in 1870 and Prussia followed suit in 1873. Educated, dedicated civil servants, the Mugwumps believed, would stand above party politics, provide capable and honest administration, and, no longer pawns of partisan politics, stay in their positions so long as they performed well.

Though nearly all Republicans, the Mugwumps acquired a reputation for breaking with their party, especially after a group of them endorsed Democrat Grover Cleveland in 1884. Such disloyalty drew the contempt of professional politicians. James G. Blaine, a perceptive and powerful Republican leader, dismissed them as "noisy but not numerous" and "pretentious but not powerful." In an age when men expected each other to exhibit a profound party loyalty, crossing party lines called into question the

Mugwumps' very gender identity. One staunch Republican derided them as "effeminate without being either masculine or feminine." Another claimed that they rode horses sidesaddle, as well-bred women did, because "there is not one among them masculine enough to ride astraddle."

In the political world of the Gilded Age, men considered women, who could not vote, to stand outside the party system. The prevailing concepts of domesticity and separate spheres dictated that women avoid politics, especially party politics. *Domesticity* was the widely shared understanding that the proper place for a woman was in a family, as wife and mother, and that the wife-mother was guardian of the family, responsible for its moral, spiritual, and physical well-being. Proponents of this view argued that women ought not experience much of the world beyond family, church, and school, because business or politics, with their sometimes lax moral standards, might corrupt women and thereby disqualify them from their vaunted and traditional roles. This was expressed in the contemporary understanding that men and women ought, most of the time, to occupy *separate spheres*. The association of political decision making with party gatherings and the proverbial smoke-filled rooms reinforced the view that politics provided no place for decent women. Thus, when it came, the movement for woman suffrage not only challenged the concept of the separate spheres but also widespread patterns of political behavior.

The struggle for woman suffrage dated to 1848, when Elizabeth Cady Stanton and four other women organized the world's first Women's Rights Convention, held at Seneca Falls, New York. The participants drafted a Declaration of Principles that announced, in part, "it is the duty of the women of this country to secure to themselves their sacred right to the elective franchise." Stanton emerged as the most prominent leader in the struggle for women's rights, especially voting rights, from 1848 to her death in 1902. She chalked up important successes in convincing lawmakers to change some laws, but she could not bring any change in laws that limited voting to men. After 1851, Susan B. Anthony became Stanton's constant partner in these efforts. During the last half of the nineteenth century, women increasingly participated in public affairs, including movements to abolish slavery, mobilize support for the Union, improve educational opportunities, and promote temperance.

In 1869, Stanton, Anthony, and their supporters formed the National Woman Suffrage Association (NWSA), its membership open only to women. Throughout most of its existence, the NWSA championed an amendment to the federal constitution as the most certain route to woman suffrage. Toward that end, Stanton and Anthony sought to build alliances with other reform and radical organizations, and they engaged in efforts to improve the status of women more generally, from promoting women's trade unions to advocating easier divorce laws and better access to information on birth control. A more conservative group, the American Woman Suffrage Association (AWSA), also organized in 1869, opened its membership to both men and women. For twenty years, the two organizations led the suffrage cause, disagreeing not on the final goal but on the best means to achieve it. They finally merged in 1890, under the leadership of Stanton, to become the National American Woman Suffrage Association.

As early as 1868, a few people had argued that woman suffrage inhered in citizenship and that the Fourteenth Amendment, in fact, had granted women the right to vote. Several hundred women tested this theory between 1868 and 1872. Voting officials turned away most of them, but a few actually voted. Some who did, including Anthony in 1872, found themselves under arrest for "illegal voting." Suffrage advocates appealed one case, involving a woman barred from registering to vote. In its decision, the Supreme Court, in 1875, confirmed that women were citizens but also specified that the Fourteenth and Fifteenth amendments had not enfranchised them.

With the Court's ruling, the NWSA focused its efforts on amending the federal constitution. In 1878, Senator A. A. Sargent of California, a friend of Anthony, first proposed such an amendment, its wording the same as that finally ratified in 1920: "The right of citizens of the United States to vote shall not be denied or abridged by the United States or any state on account of sex." Sympathetic legislators reintroduced the proposal in each new session of Congress until 1896. It reached a vote only once, in the Senate in 1887, when it lost by a vote of 16 ayes to 34 nays, with 26 absent.

The first victories for woman suffrage came, instead, at territorial and state levels in the West. In 1869, the Wyoming territorial legislature extended the franchise to women and the Republican governor approved. At the time, about 2,000 women and 7,000 men lived in Wyoming Territory, and one often-cited explanation for the men's action was that they hoped to attract more women to the territory. For the next twenty years, Wyoming women voted and served on juries and as public officials. Nonetheless, in 1889, when Wyoming sought statehood, many Congressmen balked at admitting a state that permitted women to vote. When Wyoming legislators learned that they might have to give up women suffrage in order to proceed with statehood, they replied that "We will remain out of the Union a hundred years rather than come in without the women." Congress finally voted to approve Wyoming statehood—with woman suffrage—in 1890.

The Utah territorial legislature adopted woman suffrage in 1870. Unlike in Wyoming Territory, there were nearly equal numbers of men and women in Utah Territory. There, Mormons formed the majority, and some scholars have cited the Mormons' egalitarian attitude toward women to explain woman suffrage in Utah. Others have pointed to the importance of women's votes for maintaining the power of the Mormon church in territorial politics and for defusing criticism of the Mormons' practice of polygamy, the practice of having several wives, which Mormons called plural marriage and which their religion sanctioned. In 1887, Congress passed a measure that both outlawed polygamy and disfranchised the women of Utah Territory. Not until 1896, after the Mormon church disavowed plural marriage and dissolved its political party, did Utah became a state. At that time Utah women regained the vote.

As the century waned, several states began to permit women limited voting rights, especially on nonpartisan matters, such as school-board elections and bond issues. By 1890, women could vote in school-board elections in nineteen states, and on bond and tax issues in three. In a major breakthrough for the suffrage cause, the male voters of Colorado approved woman suffrage in 1893, the first time that suffrage rights had resulted from a popular vote. Idaho's male voters endorsed woman suffrage in 1896. Despite valiant efforts by suffrage advocates (both female and male), however, between 1896 and 1910 no state passed a proposal to grant women the vote.

Obviously, the vast majority of women did not exercise the suffrage during the Gilded Age, but significant numbers of them nonetheless took an active part in the political process. The most prominent women's political organization during the Gilded Age was the Women's Christian Temperance Union (WCTU), formed in 1874 and led from 1879 to 1898 by Frances Willard, a talented organizer who had grown up on a farm, struggled for an education, and served briefly as head of a small woman's college before becoming corresponding secretary and then president of the WCTU. Dedicated to elimination of alcohol from American society, the WCTU often operated through old-stock Protestant churches. The concept of domesticity defined moral uplift and protection of the family as central duties for women, and the WCTU championed both causes in justification of its demand to ban alcohol. By the early 1890s, the WCTU claimed 150,000 members, making it the largest women's organization in the country. Some WCTU members never came close to politics, but others became deeply involved in many aspects of the political process, ranging from collecting signatures on petitions to speaking at rallies to lobbying in the corridors of state capitols. By the 1890s, other women's organizations had also begun to organize at state and national levels and to advocate changes in public policy.

By the 1880s, the WCTU had developed a close working relationship with a political party, the Prohibition party. Before the Civil War, various organizations had promoted temperance, but they had usually treated it more as a matter of individual persuasion than one for political action. Political parties dedicated to prohibition came into existence in several states in the late 1860s,

however, and a national convention created the Prohibition party
in 1869. Their platform always focused on prohibition of "the traffic in intoxicating beverages," which they called "a dishonor to
Christian civilization," but the Prohibitionists also endorsed other
reforms, including woman suffrage. The new party grew slowly,
counting only 18 state organizations in 1876. They managed to organize in 37 states by 1888, but fell back to 32 in 1892. Their
share of the national vote was tiny even during their best years, a
bit over 1 percent in 1884 and just over 2 percent in 1888 and
1892. Most of their votes were drawn from the Republicans, the
party of respectability and morality, rather than from the Democrats, the party of personal liberty. Had all the Prohibition voters in
1884 and 1888 cast their ballots for the Republicans, the Republicans would have received a plurality of the popular vote in both
those elections.

By the mid-1880s, the WCTU often acted as the female arm
of the Prohibition party. In return, in 1884 the Prohibitionists
praised the WCTU for its "purity of purpose and method" and
"earnestness, zeal, intelligence and devotion" and asserted that its
members were "eminently blessed of God." For many women, the
WCTU led them from domesticity to espousing political reform,
then to advocating woman suffrage. The WCTU endorsed woman
suffrage in 1882, the first endorsement by a major women's organization other than those created to advocate suffrage. Some
WCTU members became even more involved in politics by supporting the Prohibition party, campaigning for it, and lobbying
legislators in support of prohibition. Although some earlier historians depicted the Prohibitionists and the members of the WCTU as
backward-looking rural fanatics working out their anxiety over the
unsettling rise of an urban and industrial society, more recent studies have indicated that both groups drew significant support in urban areas and that most of their leaders were not only well-
educated, financially secure, and urban, but often pillars of their
communities.

If most leading Prohibitionists were socially respected and
economically successful, neither was true of many who led or supported one or another of the short-lived farmer or labor parties

during the 1870s and 1880s. Known variously as Reform, Independent, Anti-Monopoly, Labor, People's, or Greenback parties, they sometimes scored local victories but failed utterly to translate those local successes into a national organization capable of mounting a serious presidential campaign. Indeed, the presidential campaigns of the Greenback (1876), Greenback Labor (1880, 1884), and Union Labor (1888) parties fared so badly that they cannot provide a reliable indication of the level of support that they and similar parties could sometimes mobilize in local or state elections. Further, the granger campaigns of the late 1870s had no organizational connection with the labor parties formed in the mid-1880s. On the contrary, the scattered victories and strong showings of these disparate parties came in quite different areas and drew upon quite different coalitions of voters.

Nonetheless, the farmer and labor parties shared important concepts with the major farm and labor organizations of the era, the Grange, Farmers' Alliances, Knights of Labor, and many trade unions. Some of these parties even drew upon those organizations for some of their leadership and for much of their voter base. And, over the course of the 1870s and 1880s, these related organizations and parties developed a set of policy proposals that projected a significantly different role for government than that espoused by either the Republicans or the Democrats.

The central shared concept among farmer and labor organizations and the related parties was that of the *producing classes*, which all these groups used to specify their place in the political economy vis-à-vis other groups. Derived from the labor theory of value, this concept of class divided society into producers, those whose labor produced value, and parasites, those who fattened on the value produced by others. Producers, or wealth makers, included self-employed farmers and artisans as well as wage earners, and the concept was often extended to owners of small businesses or to professionals who came from and continued to identify with the producing classes. Parasites included bankers, lawyers, gamblers, saloon keepers, speculators, factory owners, wholesalers, and others who lived off the labor of the producers. Those who subscribed to this concept often concluded that producers

could best secure the full value of their labor through the formation of producers' and consumers' cooperatives, thereby eliminating many of the economic roles filled by bankers, wholesalers, re-
tailers, and factory owners.

Of the major organizations that subscribed to these views, the
first, chronologically, was the Grange, officially called the Patrons
of Husbandry. Oliver H. Kelley, an official in the Agriculture Department in Washington, D.C., founded the Grange in 1867 in the
hope that the organization might provide opportunities for farm
families to socialize and to learn new and more efficient methods
of agriculture. Organized as a lodge, with a secret ritual modeled
on the Masonic order, the Grange provided full participation for
women as well as men. It grew rapidly, especially in the Midwest
and the central South. In the 1870s, the Grange became a leading
proponent of cooperative buying and selling. By 1872, cooperatives
operated one-third of the grain elevators in Iowa, many of them under
Grange auspices. Two state Granges began manufacturing farm ma-
chinery, and in several other states grangers laid ambitious plans for
cooperative factories for producing a range of goods, from wagons
to sewing machines. Some grangers formed mutual insurance
companies, and a few experimented with cooperative banks.

The Grange defined itself as nonpartisan but, in the Midwest,
its meetings often turned to talk of political action. In 1873 and
1874, many Grangers took part in creating new political parties in
eleven states: Indiana, Illinois, Michigan, Wisconsin, Minnesota,
Iowa, Missouri, Kansas, Nebraska, California, and Oregon. Organized only on a state level, the new parties' names varied from
state to state—Reform, Anti-Monopoly, and Independent were
most common—but many people simply called them "granger
parties." Railroads formed a special object of concern for the new
parties, for many farmers were outraged by what they regarded as
unfair shipping costs for their produce and for manufactured
goods they had to buy. The granger parties most frequently demanded state legislation to prevent railroads from charging dis-
criminatory rates. In midwestern states, people often called such
railroad regulation "granger laws," even though local merchants
and other shippers often proved more effective than the grangers

in securing their passage. In some places, granger parties actually elected a few local and state officials, sometimes in coalition with the Democrats.

The Grange reached its zenith in the mid-1870s. Then some of their cooperatives began to experience financial difficulties. The collapse of local cooperatives often extended to local Granges. Political activity brought a few successes but also generated some bitter internal disputes. After the late 1870s, the surviving Granges usually avoided both cooperatives and politics. In the 1880s, a new set of farmers' organizations arose in the western Midwest and in the South; these were known as Farmers' Alliances. Like the Grange before them, the Alliances combined social and educational activities with promotion of producers' and consumers' cooperatives (see Chapter 3).

Some of the agricultural issues that motivated the granger parties contributed to the birth of the Greenback party in 1875 and 1876, with some granger parties, especially in Indiana and Illinois, joining in its formation. Elsewhere, connections between granger parties and Greenbackers were less clear. The Greenbackers took their name from the paper money printed during the Civil War, the increased use and supply of which, they argued, could resolve a central dilemma facing farmers. The post–Civil War era was one of *deflation*, i.e. most prices fell due to more efficient techniques in agriculture and manufacturing, the federal surplus (see Chapter 2), and to the failure of the money supply to grow as rapidly as the population. Greenbackers focused on the last of these and argued that the government could stabilize prices by printing more greenbacks. At the time, several types of paper money were in circulation. Federally chartered banks issued national bank notes based on their federal bond holdings, and the federal government issued gold certificates, which were redeemable in gold. And then there were the United States notes—the greenbacks—which could not be redeemed in gold before 1879.

At base, the Greenbackers were arguing the *quantity theory of money*: if the currency (all money in circulation) grew more rapidly than the economy, it produced *inflation* (rising prices); if the currency failed to grow as rapidly as the economy, it produced deflation (falling prices). They were also arguing for *fiat money*, in that they claimed that money has value because the government says it has value, rather than having value because it could be redeemed in a precious metal. Bankers and federal Treasury officials, however, condemned both arguments as not just fallacious but even heretical.

When Greenbackers called for the federal government to counteract falling prices by issuing more paper money, they found their most receptive audience among farmers in debt. After the Civil War, farmers, especially in the Midwest and the South, rapidly increased their production of the leading commercial crops. Land planted to corn, wheat, and cotton more than tripled, and new farming methods greatly increased harvests of these agricultural commodities. As Table 1.1 shows, as production rose, prices fell. Farmers had accomplished much of their expansion on borrowed money—to buy land, supplies, seeds, implements, and livestock, and even to live on until the first harvest.

Indebtedness was widespread among farmers, especially in the Midwest and South, and the money to make their loan payments came almost entirely from the sale of their crops. Falling crop prices effectively magnified their debt. At the time, loans were not amortized, so a farmer who borrowed $1,000 for five years expected to pay interest each year on the entire sum and to repay the full $1,000 at the end of five years. In 1881, corn sold for 63 cents per bushel, at best, so a $1,000 loan taken out that year was equivalent to 1,587 bushels of corn. In 1886, when the loan came due, corn sold for 36 cents per bushel, so $1,000 required 2,777 bushels. Ten percent interest would have cost $100 per year—equivalent to 159 bushels of corn in 1881 but to 312 in 1885. Falling prices pushed farmers to raise more and more each year just to cover interest and loans, and the more they raised, the lower prices fell. Like the character in *Alice in Wonderland*, they had to run faster and faster just to stay in the same place. It is not surprising, thus, that many farmers readily embraced the Greenbackers' promise of an expanded money supply that would drive up the prices they received for their crops.

The Greenbackers, however, were never a single-interest party. In 1880 and 1884, their platforms called for the protection of laborers, the eight-hour day for government employees, health and safety regulations for workplaces, implementation of a graduated income tax (which, it was argued, would tax both the rich and the poor fairly), and regulation of interstate commerce, especially the railroads. They also opposed the use of child labor and the disfranchisement of African Americans in the South. In some of their platforms, they seemed to sympathize with woman suffrage, but they never endorsed it outright.

In the 1878 congressional elections, the Greenback party received over a million votes and elected several members of the House of Representatives. In the 1880 presidential election, they nominated as their standard-bearer James B. Weaver of Iowa, a Greenback congressman who had been a Union general during the Civil War. Weaver got a bit over 3 percent of the popular vote. In 1884, with a similar platform and the erratic Benjamin Butler, another former Union general, as their presidential nominee, the Greenbackers did even worse, receiving less than 2 percent.

Throughout the 1880s, Greenbackers often allied themselves with local or state labor parties. Labor parties had appeared as early as the Jacksonian era, and the National Labor Union tried to form a political party in 1872. Local labor parties appeared in a number of cities and towns throughout the 1870s and 1880s. Their high point, in 1886, coincided with the high point for membership in the Knights of Labor. The Knights grew out of an organization of Philadelphia garment workers. Reorganized in 1869, they proclaimed that labor was "the only creator of values or capital" and opened their ranks to all members of "the producing class." Led by Terence V. Powderly from 1879 to 1893, the Knights emphasized organization, education, and cooperation as the chief objectives of their order. They favored political action to accomplish a range of labor reforms, including workplace health and safety laws, the eight-hour day, prohibition of child labor, equal pay for equal work regardless of gender, and the graduated income tax. In many towns and cities, the growth of the Knights stimulated emergence of local labor parties, just as the growth of the Grange had sparked the creation of the granger parties.

In 1886, the Independent Labor party of New York City nominated Henry George, a well-known journalist and reformer, for mayor. With backing from trade unions and the Knights of Labor, and a strong appeal to New York's Irish community, George polled 31 percent of the vote, finished second to the Democratic candidate who received 41 percent, and trounced the Republican candidate, young Theodore Roosevelt. That same year, the United Labor party of Chicago drew 27 percent of the vote for county treasurer, and an independent party with labor backing won the mayoralty in Milwaukee. Labor parties also made strong showings in other communities in the mid-1880s.

The successes of urban labor parties in 1886 encouraged Greenbackers, members of farm organizations, and labor party activists to seek a coalition for the 1888 presidential election. Early in 1887 they united to form the Union Labor party and tried to appeal to discontented farmers and urban workers. The new party chose Anson J. Streeter, head of the northern Farmers' Alliance, as its candidate for president and produced a more radical platform than its labor party predecessors. Claiming to speak for "the wealth-producer," the party reiterated many Greenback, labor, and granger proposals. The new party went further and added a demand for government ownership of the means of transportation and communication. In the election, however, the Union Labor party did even worse than the Greenbackers had on their own, drawing just over 1 percent of the vote, even less than the Prohibitionists. Thus, throughout the 1880s, farmer and labor parties proved far more potent in local elections than in national contests, and their efforts to fuse rural and urban protest into a viable single party consistently failed.

The various groups and parties on the periphery of Gilded Age politics might have shared an alienation from the major parties, but they also differed greatly among themselves. Mugwumps espoused laissez-faire economics and scorned the grangers' calls for regulation and the Greenbackers' demands for inflation. Many Mugwumps also opposed woman suffrage. The suffragists and the prohibitionists both faced internal divisions over tactics, whether to focus narrowly on a single issue or form coalitions with other reform groups. Some unionists disapproved of labor parties, especially leaders of unions affiliated with the new AFL, formed in 1886. Other labor activists, especially those from the Knights of Labor, helped to form and lead the labor parties.

By the late 1880s, all of the peripheral groups agreed on only one point—the need to reform prevailing voting practices by instituting the "Australian ballot," a voting system whereby: the government printed and distributed ballots; the ballot listed all candidates; and the voter marked the ballot secretly, in a private voting booth. Developed first in Australia in the 1850s and subsequently adopted in Great Britain and Canada, the system began to attract attention in the United States when Henry George described it in a leading journal in 1883. The idea developed widespread support not only from groups on the periphery of politics, but also from many members of the major parties. In early 1888, with only a single dissenting vote, the Kentucky legislature, composed mostly of Democrats, approved the nation's first Australian ballot law, but it applied only to the city of Louisville. Later that year the Massachusetts legislature, mostly Republicans, adopted it for all elections in the state, and several other states approved it in 1889. By the 1892 presidential election, nearly all states outside the South had adopted it.

In some southern states, beginning with Tennessee in 1889, the dominant Democrats recognized that the secret ballot could function as a de facto literacy test, disproportionately disfranchising many blacks and hill-country whites who had very few educational opportunities and who usually voted Republican. The Republicans of Massachusetts may also have understood that a system that isolated the voter in a booth and required him to read and understand a written document in a relatively short time might disfranchise at least some of the poor Boston Irish who usually voted Democratic. Thus, the reformers, who had hoped to make it harder to manipulate voters at the polls, won support for the secret ballot from some members of the major parties eager to disfranchise opposition voters.

This change in the voting system carried important implications for political parties. No longer could party activists see which party's ballot a voter dropped into the ballot box. No longer would voters find it difficult to vote a "split ticket." No longer did a party require an army of campaign workers to distribute ballots. Now the candidates of tiny parties—or even individuals with no party backing at all—could run for office and know that every voter would receive a ballot listing their names. Using the secret ballot as their battering ram, reformers had forced a major opening in the formidable wall that parties had built around every part of the political process.

The secret ballot was a new element in the politics of the Gilded Age, but many others dated to the years before the Civil War. The Democrats liked to trace their origins to the 1790s, but they really emerged in their nineteenth-century form in the 1830s. Republicans first organized their party in the 1850s. Thus, throughout the late nineteenth century, the origins of the two parties were within the memory of at least some current participants in the political process. Many of the characteristics of party politics during the Gilded Age also had originated in the third of a century preceding the Civil War—the mass-based parties, conventions and platforms, campaigning styles, and the spoils system. The basic party orientations also sprang from pre–Civil War roots. Most characteristics of the state, too, came from the generation that preceded the Gilded Age, although during the Civil War and Reconstruction the Republicans had enacted substantial changes in the nature of citizenship and in federal economic policy.

From the mid-1870s to the 1890s, the two major parties were in such close balance that there was no national majority party and neither party could easily enact its proposals into law. Party politics seemed to freeze into deadlock. The parties themselves seemed to freeze as well, changing very little from what they had become during the politically volatile 1850s and 1860s. In the last decade of the century, however, politics entered a period of upheaval, when nearly all elements of politics not only unfroze but changed in profound ways.

CHAPTER TWO

The Deadlock of National
Politics, 1868–1890

Many historians have seen the politics of the Gilded Age as dead-locked—frozen in place, with little governmental reaction to the far-reaching transformation of the economy and society then in progress. And, as already noted, many elements in the political system changed little or not at all during those years. Yet, para-doxically, these decades also included extraordinarily high levels of participation in voting, intense party loyalties, and overflowing attendance at political parades and rallies. The ardent public par-ticipation in local political revelry and the high level of voting turnout, together with the absence of significant changes in federal economic policy, led some earlier historians to condemn the grass-roots activities as mere circuses thrown by the parties to distract voters from what those same historians considered the "real is-sues" of regulating emerging corporate power. A more complex understanding of this twenty-year deadlock, however, must take into account the close competition between the two major parties, the way that the prevailing political culture defined the roles of Congress and president relative to each other, the specific circumstances that blocked parties' efforts to take action when the impasse momentarily lifted, and the important new policies that emerged despite the supposed "deadlock."

From the mid-1870s to the mid-1890s, competition between the Republicans and Democrats at the national level was very close. (Table 2.1 presents the popular vote and electoral vote for these years.) Although the popular presidential vote was consistently very close, the electoral vote appears more decisive—but those margins are deceptive. In 1880, 1884, and 1888, the electoral votes of New York state were cast for the winning candidate. Had the other candidate carried New York in any of those contests, he would have won—and New York was very closely balanced between the two major parties. In those three elections, the winner and loser were, in effect, separated by only 1 or 2 percent of the New York state vote.

After the mid-1870s, certain realities of Electoral College arithmetic quickly become apparent. (Table 2.2 summarizes the Electoral College vote for Democratic strongholds and for the closely competitive states of New York, Indiana, and Connecticut.) To win, a Democratic presidential candidate needed only to win the usual Democratic strongholds plus New York and one or both of the other "swing" states. Such arithmetic makes clear why the Democrats nominated New Yorkers for their presidential candidates four times out of five between 1872 and 1888, and why they turned to Indianans for vice-presidential candidates three times during those same years. Furthermore, Ohio and Illinois could be nearly as competitive as Indiana. For the Republicans to win, they had to hold all three of those midwestern states. Not surprisingly, four of the five Republican presidential candidates came from Illinois, Indiana, or Ohio. Just as the Democrats usually nominated midwesterners for vice-president, so the Republicans usually nominated New Yorkers for that spot. Although most presidential elections were very close, and despite the Democrats' seeming advantage, the Republicans usually won in the Electoral College, even when they lost the popular vote. Democrats received the most popular votes in four of the six presidential elections beginning in 1876, but they won the most electoral votes in only two of them, a circumstance deriving from the large popular margins that Democrats customarily received in winning the relatively sparse electoral votes of the southern and border states as compared to much narrower popular margins for the Republicans in northern states that were richer in electoral votes.

Though Democrats rarely won the presidency, they usually held a majority in the House of Representatives. (Table 2.3 summarizes party strength in Congress.) The Democrats' House majority, however, was sometimes so small that a dozen absent members could wipe it out. Republicans were usually in the majority in the Senate, but there, too, the majority was usually very small. During the eleven sessions of Congress between 1875 and 1897, the Republicans controlled both houses of Congress and the presidency at the same time only twice, in 1881–1883 and 1889–1891.[1] Only once during those eleven Congresses, in 1893–1895, did Democrats control the House, Senate, and White House at the same time.

Given the climate of close competition and intense party loyalty characteristic of Gilded Age politics, any effort to push through a *party* agenda was probably destined to fail because any new legislation required approval by House, Senate, and president. The Republican majority in the Senate could usually block any Democratic proposal, and the Democratic majority in the House of Representatives could similarly block any proposal by the Republicans. The difficulties that both parties faced in mustering a ma-

---

1 The Constitution, Article 1, Section 4, specifies that Congress shall meet at least once each year beginning on the first Monday in December. (In 1933, this provision was superseded by the Twentieth Amendment, which specifies January 3rd.) Throughout the Gilded Age, members elected to Congress in November typically waited thirteen months before beginning their service unless a special session was called to meet earlier. The second session usually began following the next elections for members of the House and was often called the "lame duck" session because it included some members who had just been rejected by the voters. The famous Fifty-first Congress, for example, was elected in November 1888 and met for its first session from December 1889 to October 1890. Elections were then held in November 1890, and the second session of the Fifty-first Congress met in December 1890, even though many of its Republican members had lost their reelection campaigns the month before.

jority for their proposals in both houses thus contributed in significant ways to the freezing of most federal policies during the Gilded Age.

Factors deriving from the broader political culture, beyond electoral and congressional arithmetic, also contributed to the deadlock. Leaders in both parties held attitudes toward the presidency that made it improbable that a president would seek a significant leadership role in policy making. Abraham Lincoln had assumed immense presidential powers during the Civil War, but, for a generation, none of his successors in the White House wielded anything approaching Lincoln's power. Lincoln's vice-president and successor, Andrew Johnson, struggled with the Republicans in Congress over control of Reconstruction policy, and lost the contest. The outcome tipped the balance of power from the presidency to the Congress, and the presidents who came after Johnson did little to challenge congressional dominance.

This situation met with approval from many prominent Republicans. John Sherman, a highly influential Republican who spent nearly fifty years in the House and Senate and as Secretary of the Treasury and Secretary of State, stated a Whiggish view that most Republicans probably shared: the executive "should be subordinate to the legislative department." George Hoar, who represented Massachusetts in Congress for many years, recalled that he had often visited the White House to *give* advice but never to *receive* it. A midwestern Republican governor in 1881 elaborated on this concept of a limited executive when he defined his duties as "to secure the effective enforcement of law, and to guard the interests of the state so as to avoid useless expenditures, and encourage frugality in the management of the state institutions." Many Republicans also considered cabinet members as virtually autonomous, subject to congressional oversight but not presidential control.

Cleveland, the lone Democrat to serve in the White House between 1861 and 1913, also espoused a restricted notion of the presidency and tried to avoid what he considered "interference with the legislative branch and its constitutional responsibilities." Nonetheless, his view of the presidency did differ from that of his

Republican contemporaries. Like many Democrats, he drew upon the heritage of Andrew Jackson to define the role of the president as restraining the recklessness and extravagance of Congress through vetoes. He insisted that the government not dole out "direct and especial favors," and he used his veto power unsparingly to stop such measures—414 times during his first administration alone, compared with 205 by all his predecessors in the presidency! Though willing, even eager, to assert the power of the presidency by vetoing congressional actions, Cleveland provided little positive party leadership.

Both the Whiggish Republican view of the presidency and the Jacksonian Democratic concept are very different from twentieth-century expectations that the president should be the major policy initiator, or "chief legislator," preparing bills and lobbying Congress to pass them. Throughout the Gilded Age, presidents supplied little domestic policy leadership beyond sending Congress an annual report that contained suggestions for legislative action. Virtually no one expected the president to play the role of chief legislator, and no president between 1865 and 1889 did so.

The intensely partisan nature of nearly all political decision making, the close balance between Republicans and Democrats, and the widespread expectation that the president should not be a policy initiator all contributed to the freezing of much federal domestic policy after the end of Reconstruction. Nonetheless, significant changes did appear. A survey of presidential administrations from Grant through Harrison will indicate the long-term continuities and the few important policy innovations, as well as the difficulties facing those who sought to create new policies and the bipartisan nature of most major policy changes.

Grant: The Emergence of Deadlock, 1868–1876

Shortly before Ulysses S. Grant won the presidency for the Republicans in 1868, Congress had wrested control of domestic policy, especially Reconstruction, away from President Andrew Johnson and had tried unsuccessfully to remove him from office. Congressional dominance over much of domestic policy continued with Grant in the White House.

During Grant's presidency, Congress passed the last significant Reconstruction legislation: the Enforcement Acts of 1870 and 1871, intended to suppress the Ku Klux Klan and similar terrorist organizations, and the Civil Rights Act of 1875, which prohibited racial discrimination in such public places as restaurants, theaters, and railroad coaches. In passing these measures, Congress took the initiative and Grant did little. Indeed, at one point in the House discussion of the Enforcement Act of 1871, Congressman James Garfield complained that "The President, it is said, greatly desires legislation but hesitates to recommend it." Grant eventually wrote to Congress urging approval of the bill but, like most Gilded Age presidents, limited himself to a formal communication and did little else to secure the its passage. Congress approved the Civil Rights Act of 1875 despite Grant's announced opposition. He once threatened to veto it but eventually signed it after removal of some features he found objectionable.

Grant directly challenged Congress in only one area. In 1869, shortly before his inauguration, he met with a group of Quakers who persuaded him to launch a new "Peace Policy" for American Indians. In fact, this approach constituted not so much a clearly delineated alternative to existing policy as a set of decisions that, together, were called the "Peace Policy." As Commissioner of Indian Affairs, Grant appointed a general who had served on his military staff since early in the Civil War—Ely S. Parker, also known as Donehogawa, a lawyer and engineer and also a chief of the Senecas and Grand Sachem of the Iroquois Confederation. Parker was the first American Indian to serve as Commissioner of Indian Affairs. As part of his new policy, Grant removed some Indian Affairs appointments from the spoils system and filled those positions instead with officials recommended by leading Protestant church organizations. His real objective, however, was to give administration of most Indian affairs to the army. Disgruntled over losing patronage posts to religious groups but recognizing the political folly of criticizing churches, Congress struck back at Grant by flatly prohibiting any role for the army in the Indian Affairs office. Grant, however, did not return the contested posts to the spoils system but instead had the churches fill them too. In this, as in most matters, however, Grant was inconsistent; toward the end of his administration, he appointed as Secretary of the Interior (including Indian Affairs) one of his party's most practiced spoilsmen, Zachariah Chandler.

The central goal of Grant's Peace Policy, a goal shared by nearly all whites who advocated reform of federal Indian policy, was assimilation—the elimination of Indian cultural distinctiveness in an effort to bring them into the mainstream of American life and to terminate their special legal status as sovereign dependent nations, whether or not they wanted to change. Grant sought to end the practice of negotiating treaties with Indian tribes and, thereby, to move toward ending their status as autonomous political entities. Congress endorsed that approach in legislation passed in 1871, but that action owed as much to House jealousy of Senate treaty prerogatives as to a reasoned commitment to a new policy. Grant and the reformers also intended that Indians should become wards of the federal state, and that, as wards of the state, they should receive the education, training, and supplies that would prepare them for assimilation.

Though he took pride in his "Peace Policy," Grant was always prepared to use military force to keep Indians on the reservations where the assimilation process was presumably to begin. Toward the end of his presidency, this led to the last major U.S.-Indian wars: in 1874–75 on the southern Great Plains, and in 1876–77 on the northern Plains. These campaigns defeated the Indians of both regions, even though on June 25, 1876, a large group of Lakota and Cheyenne warriors led by Crazy Horse and Sitting Bull wiped out Colonel George A. Custer and some 250 men of the Seventh Cavalry.

Grant's efforts to change federal Indian policy pleased some reformers, but he disappointed others when he failed to follow through on early expressions of sympathy for civil service reform. He also alienated some prominent Republicans by failing to consult with party leaders on appointments. Indeed, the dogged determination that had made Grant a winning general seemed to be in short supply in President Grant. He often proved to be weak, unassertive, easily influenced, even manipulated—qualities that prevented him from being a good, or even a satisfactory chief executive. Not only did he fail to consult with leaders of his party over major appointments, he sometimes appointed his friends or acquaintances to government positions for which they possessed no particular qualifications. Partly as a consequence, he faced constant turnover in his cabinet—five attorneys general (more than any other president), five secretaries of war (also a record), and four treasury secretaries. Grant did appoint a highly capable secretary of state, Hamilton Fish, and he eventually found a secretary of the treasury, Benjamin Bristow, who vigorously routed out corruption. Some of Grant's appointees, however, seemed to view their positions primarily as the spoils of party victory, and revelations of corruption were not long in coming.

Although the most serious scandals of his administration came in Grant's second term, his failure to provide party leadership contributed to a party schism as he ran for reelection in 1872. A "Liberal Republican" movement attracted Republicans who opposed the Grant administration or the dominant Republican faction in Congress for a variety of reasons—distaste for some Reconstruction measures, support for civil service reform, or opposition to high tariffs. The Liberal Republicans split with their party and held their own nominating convention. Horace Greeley, influential editor of the New York *Tribune* and an erstwhile Republican, won the Liberals' nomination for president.

Greeley had been an ardent opponent of slavery before the Civil War and had given strong support to the passage of the Fourteenth and Fifteenth amendments, but he had taken puzzling positions at times in his forty-year career, including a willingness to let the South secede in 1860–1861. One political observer described Greeley as "so conceited, fussy, and foolish that he damages every cause he wants to support." His unkempt appearance conveyed little of a presidential image, and the caustic pen of Thomas Nast, cartoonist for *Harper's Weekly*, transformed Greeley into a befuddled caricature. Greeley had long scourged the Democrats in his newspaper, but they now found common ground in opposing high tariffs and the continuation of Reconstruction. Democrats accordingly made Greeley their presidential nominee in an effort to unite the forces opposing Grant. Given Greeley's stance on nearly every issue, most voters seem to have understood the Democrats' action as pure opportunism. Grant won convincingly, with nearly 56 percent of the vote, demonstrating his own personal popularity, Greeley's weakness as a candidate, and the continuing Republican loyalties of most voters.

Soon after the 1872 election, an investigation revealed that four years before, before Grant became president, several prominent congressional leaders had accepted stock in the Crédit Mobilier. The chief shareholders of the Union Pacific Railroad had created the Crédit Mobilier as a construction company, and they gave it a very generous contract to build the railroad. The chief shareholders in the Union Pacific thereby paid themselves handsomely for constructing their railroad. To protect this arrangement from congressional scrutiny, the company sold shares cheaply to key members of Congress, who then shared in the company's inflated profits. Those politicians involved included the two men who served as vice-president under Grant. After Democratic campaigners used rumors about the arrangement to embarrass more than a dozen Republicans in the 1872 elections, Congress began an investigation. Leading Republicans were implicated, and the Republican congressional leaders carefully managed the investigation to deflect attention from all but those most directly involved. The investigating committee concluded that several, including future president James A. Garfield, had been indiscreet but had acted without corrupt intent—a valid judgment with regard to Garfield and probably some of the others. The committee caught former vice-president Schuyler Colfax in so many contradictions that his political career was destroyed. Contradictions abounded in and between the testimonies of other witnesses, too, suggesting that some of them were either confused or lying. Withal, the committee found no direct evidence of bribery, but the House censured two representatives, one Republican and one Democrat, for their actions.

No sooner did that scandal quiet down than Congress—with Republican majorities in both houses—voted itself a 50 percent increase in pay and made it two years retroactive. Only after widespread public protest did Congress repeal what had been dubbed the "salary grab."

In 1875, Treasury Secretary Bristow discovered widespread corruption in the collection of whiskey taxes. A "Whiskey Ring" of federal officials and distillers, centered in St. Louis, had conspired to enable the manufacturers to evade payment of the federal tax on distilled liquor. The 230 men indicted included several of Grant's appointees and even his private secretary, Orville E. Babcock. Babcock apparently persuaded Grant of his innocence, however, and Grant helped him to avoid conviction. Partly as a result, relations between Grant and Bristow deteriorated, and Bristow eventually resigned. The next year, William Belknap, Grant's secretary of war, resigned in the face of impeachment charges for accepting a bribe. Early during his administration of the War Department, his wife had arranged an annual bribe from the operator of a trading post in Indian Territory, and Belknap had continued to accept the payments after his wife's death. Grant, at the end of his presidency, admitted that "mistakes have been made" but seemed to shrug them off as due to his lack of political experience.

During Grant's stay in the White House, corruption and scandal was not limited to the federal government. In a series of exposés culminating in 1871, the press of New York City and the vitriolic cartoons of Thomas Nast in *Harper's Weekly* brought the downfall of William Marcy Tweed, leader of the "Tweed Ring," which had dominated city and state politics for several years. By controlling the city's Democratic party, Tweed and his associates controlled city government in the late 1860s and early 1870s and, for a briefer period, state government. They used their political power to channel public funds to legitimate civic and charitable organizations and also to approve major new construction projects—and they received kickbacks from the building contractors who did the work. It is estimated that the Tweed Ring may have taken as much as $200 million from the city and state and from those who did business with the city. Other scandals eventually drove the Tweed Ring's excesses from the front pages, as exposés and allegations of corruption became staples in political campaigning from New York to Mississippi to California. Railroad companies often figured in such revelations, for some of them tried to secure favorable treatment by bribing public officials, and all too many officeholders—North, South, and West—accepted their offers.

Conditions in the South seemed particularly inviting to political corruption, as Reconstruction governments rapidly expanded the realm of state responsibility and, in the process, sometimes created opportunities for the ambitious and unscrupulous. Reconstruction governments included many men—white and black alike—who had only modest holdings of their own and aspired to better things. One South Carolina legislator bluntly described his attitude toward electing a U.S. senator: "I was pretty hard up, and I did not care who the candidate was if I got two hundred dollars." But in the South, as elsewhere, corruption was nonpartisan—if Republicans seemed more prominent in their dubious achievements, it was only because they held the most important and visible offices. Accusations of Republican corruption, however, provided southern Democrats with ammunition in their tireless campaign to discredit Reconstruction leaders. In the North, support for the Reconstruction governments waned to the point where even some Republicans ceased to defend them. The Republican governor of South Carolina understood this when he observed that "The North is *tired* of the Southern question, and wants a settlement, no matter what."

Between the presidential elections of 1872 and 1876, southern politics became ever more polarized along racial lines. Intimidation and even terrorism directed against black Republicans and their remaining white allies played a role in the victory of some southern Democrats. In communities with large numbers of black Republicans, Democrats formed "rifle clubs" and held public drills with their weapons. The message was clear: black Republicans who insisted on exercising their political rights put themselves in danger. In some areas, armed whites prevented African Americans from voting. Some black Republican leaders were beaten or even killed in 1874, the year in which Democrats won over two-thirds of the South's seats in the House of Representatives and "redeemed" Alabama, Arkansas, and Texas from Republican rule.

Republican candidates in 1874 also lost in many parts of the North, due to the economic depression that began in 1873 and to the repeated scandals of the Grant administration. Before the 1874 elections, the House of Representatives was two-to-one Republican; after the 1874 elections, Democrats outnumbered Republicans by 169 to 109. Now southern Republicans could no longer look to Congress for assistance, for the Democratic majority in the House could block their legislative proposals as well as their requests for appropriations to fund their current policies. Thus, Reconstruction came to an end, and the twenty-year partisan stalemate began.

Political violence in the South accelerated, reaching such an extreme during 1875 in Mississippi that the use of terror to overthrow Reconstruction governments came to be dubbed "the Mississippi Plan." Democratic rifle clubs operated with impunity, breaking up Republican meetings and attacking Republican leaders in broad daylight. One black Mississippian described the campaign of 1875 as "the most violent time we have ever seen." In one particularly violent act of political terrorism, in Yazoo County, Mississippi, armed whites drove out the Republican sheriff and murdered several prominent black Republicans including a member of the state legislature. Local Republicans anxiously requested help from the Republican governor, Adelbert Ames. "Send help, help, troops," read one message, and another asked plaintively, "Gov., aint the[re] no pertiction?" Ames sought federal intervention, but midwestern Republicans cautioned Grant that public sentiment had so turned against military action to protect Republican state governments in the South that further intervention might defeat Republican candidates in the Midwest. Grant abandoned the Republicans of Mississippi. There was to be no federal protection.

The terror produced the desired result. In Yazoo County, for example, there were only seven Republican votes, down from several thousand. Democrats swept the balloting throughout the state, winning four-fifths of the seats in the state legislature. Once in session, the newly elected Mississippi legislature impeached and removed from office the black Republican lieutenant governor, then brought impeachment charges against Governor Ames, who re-signed and left the state. Ames had foreseen the result during the campaign when he wrote: "a *revolution* has taken place—by force of arms."

In 1876, on the centennial of American independence, the na-tion stumbled through the most troubled—and potentially danger-ous—presidential election since 1860, when the outcome of the contest had precipitated secession and civil war. As revelations of political corruption grew in both North and South, the issue of honesty and reform in government took center stage. This clouded the campaign of the leading contender for the Republican nomina-tion, James G. Blaine of Maine, a powerful member of Congress, for he may have profited from prorailroad legislation he helped to pass. The Republicans instead nominated Rutherford B. Hayes, the governor of Ohio and a former Union Army officer. At the end of the Civil War, a disproportionate number of Ohio Republicans emerged into national leadership, among them John Sherman, James Garfield, and William McKinley. Like his fellow Ohioans, Hayes demonstrated a solid grasp of party politics and a commit-ment to Republican party ideals tempered by an understanding of the need for compromise. One close associate described Hayes's "chief excellence" as "his intuitive perception of what at the mo-ment is practicably attainable." Virtually unknown outside Ohio, Hayes's unblemished reputation proved to be his greatest asset—here was a candidate "nobody could object to." The Democratic party nominated Governor Samuel J. Tilden of New York as their presidential candidate. A wealthy lawyer and businessman with a Jacksonian's dislike for big business and distrust of government, Tilden had earned a reputation as a reformer by taking a leading role, as a private citizen, in organizing other citizens against the notorious Tweed Ring and in gathering and presenting evidence against Tweed—activities that helped to secure his election as governor of New York in 1874.

First election reports indicated a Tilden victory, as he received 51 percent of the popular vote to 48 percent for Hayes. Tilden secured majorities in New York, New Jersey, and Indiana, and seemed to have carried all the border states and the South. In

South Carolina, Florida, and Louisiana, however, Republicans controlled the counting and reporting of ballots. Charging that Democrats had committed voting fraud in those states, Republican election boards invalidated enough ballots to give Hayes majorities in those three states. In Louisiana, the Republican head of the state election board simply put the state's electoral votes on the auction block, asking the Democrats for a bribe of $250,000, and later for $1 million, before reducing his price to $200,000. In the end, the official Louisiana tally went to Hayes. These states gave Hayes a one-vote margin of victory in the Electoral College. Democrats cried fraud and, in all three states, Democratic officials submitted their own versions of the "official" vote count. In addition, the Democratic governor of Oregon, where Hayes won an unquestioned majority, certified a Democratic elector in place of a Republican elector who, the governor claimed, was ineligible—thereby creating the possibility of switching the one-vote margin to Tilden's favor. Some Democrats vowed to see Tilden inaugurated by force if necessary, and some Democratic newspapers ran headlines that read: "Tilden or War."

For the first time, Congress had to face the problem of contested electoral votes that could decide the outcome of an election. To resolve the challenges, Congress, after long deliberation, created a fifteen-member Electoral Commission: five senators, five representatives, and five Supreme Court justices. By party, the commission consisted of eight Republicans and seven Democrats. Initially, the balance stood at seven to seven with one independent from the Supreme Court, but he withdrew and a Republican replaced him.

Democrats and Republicans braced themselves for a confrontation that might have turned violent. However, as the commission hearings droned on through January and into February 1877, informal discussions took place across Washington among leading Republicans and Democrats, resulting in what has long been called the "Compromise of 1877." Southern Democrats wanted "Home Rule," meaning no more federal intervention, especially military intervention, to protect the civil rights of southern blacks. They also sought representation in the cabinet, a share of federal patronage, and federal subsidies for railroad construction and waterways in the South. In return, southern Democrats were willing to abandon Tilden's claim to the White House. Other claims were made, and other arrangements whispered, but these were the central elements most often discussed. Though there was no single agreement or mutually agreed-upon set of terms for resolving the dispute, enough Republicans and enough southern Democrats eventually felt satisfied with the informal understandings they had reached. When the commission voted along party lines to confirm the election of Hayes, there was no official challenge from the Democrats.

Hayes: The Confirmation of Deadlock, 1876–1880

Hayes took office without opposition, and he soon ended the last phases of Reconstruction. He also named a former Confederate, and Democrat, to his cabinet as Postmaster General, the official responsible for the largest number of patronage appointments in the federal government. With this appointment, Hayes quickly managed to antagonize Republicans who believed that spoils should go to the victors.

Among those most critical of Hayes was Roscoe Conkling, the flamboyant Senator from New York state and the boss of that state's large and hungry Republican organization. Conkling had hoped to be the Republican nominee in 1876, and he saw little reason to assist Hayes now. Within the Republican party, Conkling could often count on the support of J. Donald Cameron, his counterpart in Pennsylvania, and John Logan, who filled a similar role in Illinois. Another contender for the 1876 nomination had been James G. Blaine, now Senator from Maine, a spellbinding orator with a capacity for winning loyal supporters and creating bitter enemies. Conkling, who saw Blaine as his chief competitor for party leadership, fell into the second category. Few major differences of policy separated Conkling from Blaine, though Conkling showed more commitment to the spoils system and to the defense of southern black voters, and Blaine took more interest in the protective tariff and Republican economic policies that encouraged industrialization and western economic development.

Though choosing a southern Democrat for Postmaster General ran the risk of completely alienating Republican spoilsmen like Conkling, it fit into a larger objective of Hayes and his supporters: to build a new and different Republican party in the South. Hayes hoped to create a viable southern Republican party based on pre–Civil War Whigs—"the same class of men," as John Sherman put it, who were Republicans in the North, that is, men "interested in industry and property." Such hopes proved unrealistic. The end of federal intervention in the South in fact marked a long-term retreat from the Republicans' commitment to protect "equality before the law" for all citizens. Republicans continued to condemn violations of black rights, but Democratic control of the House meant that any new Enforcement Act stood no chance of passage. The recurring Republican lamentations, therefore, were more of a symbolic nod to their party's heritage and an appeal for the votes of African Americans than a real commitment to action. Most Republicans seemed to understand that they had lost their southern wing with Reconstruction's demise, and they had little hope of recovering it.

The last three Republican state governments in the South fell in 1877, completing "Redemption." The Democrats, the self-described party of white supremacy, now held sway in every southern state capital. One Republican journal bitterly concluded that African Americans had been forced "to relinquish the artificial right to vote for the natural right to live." In parts of the South thereafter, election fraud and violence became routine. By 1890, one Mississippi judge acknowledged that "since 1875 . . . we have been preserving the ascendancy of the white people by . . . stuffing ballot boxes, committing perjury[,] and here and there in the state carrying the elections by fraud and violence."

Throughout Hayes's four years in office, he faced hostile Democratic majorities in the House of Representatives, and Democratic party leaders repeatedly harped on the legitimacy of his election. Nonetheless, his presidency produced several important actions or measures. In addition, his own integrity and principled stand on issues helped to restore the reputation of the Republican party after the embarrassing scandals of the Grant administration. In his inaugural address, Hayes called for civil service reform, but the members of the House and Senate posed significant impediments to any effort to modify the patronage system. Hayes even undercut his own stance that appointments should be based on ability rather than party loyalty when he rewarded some of his own supporters with appointments. Then, in a direct challenge to Conkling, Hayes tried to replace several members of the senator's organization who held key patronage positions in the New York Customhouse, including the head of that agency, Chester A. Arthur.[2] Hayes asked Arthur and one other high official to resign, but they refused. Hayes thereupon sent nominations for their replacements to the Senate, but Conkling defeated them. Hayes waited until Congress was in recess, then dismissed the two and named temporary replacements for them. Despite efforts by Conkling, the Senate eventually approved the president's choices, thereby confirming Hayes's argument that the president controlled the most important federal appointments, not local party leaders. However, in the process, he alienated both the spoilsmen, who supported Conkling's argument that local and state party leaders should be able to name those appointed to federal jobs within their bailiwicks, and those Republicans who advocated some reform of the civil service, who wanted appointments to be based on merit rather than party loyalty.

Hayes had been president for only four months when, for the first time, the nation witnessed labor strife on a national scale. In response to the depression that began in 1873, railroad companies had repeatedly cut their workers' pay. In mid-July 1877, after yet another pay cut, Baltimore and Ohio (B&O) workers in Martinsburg, West Virginia, stopped work, closing the B&O main line.

---

2 Customhouses, agencies of the Treasury Department, were located in all major ports for the collection of tariffs on imported goods. New York was the largest port in the country, and its customhouse collected more revenue than all other ports combined. The collector of the Port of New York—the head of the New York Customhouse—was paid more than the secretary of the treasury and controlled a small army of patronage appointments.

The governor sent in the state militia. One striker was killed in an exchange of gunfire, but the militia failed to end the shutdown. The governor then requested federal troops. Hayes was reluctant to intervene, but he dispatched U.S. troops when assured that state officials could not control matters and that the strikers threatened life and property. Now under the protection of federal troops as well as state militia and local authorities, strikebreakers began to operate the trains once again.

But the end of the B&O strike did not end the matter. Strikes and demonstrations against railroad companies now erupted throughout the middle Atlantic and midwestern states. In Pittsburgh, on July 21, a battle between state militia and strike supporters left twenty-four dead. After forcing the militia to retreat, strikers and strike sympathizers burned and looted railroad property throughout the city. The strike also began to spread to other workers, including those in Pittsburgh area steel mills. Tom Scott, head of the Pennsylvania Railroad, asked Hayes to take action to end the strike. Concerned about the improper use of federal troops, the president eventually deployed U.S. troops in several states but ordered them only to protect federal property and to promote "peace and order." In a few places, the soldiers also dispersed crowds of demonstrators. Hayes was concerned that federal forces be used only to prevent violence and protect life and property. The presence of a few federal troops, however, combined with local and state actions to bring the strike to an end. Most of the work stoppages and demonstrations had ended by July 31, leaving scores dead—perhaps a hundred all told—and some $10 million of damage to railroad property.

Hayes was not the first president to use federal forces to maintain order during a strike, but he usually receives credit for a precedent that was to be repeated as the nation adjusted to its new and sometimes uncomfortable role as an industrial society. Court orders against strikers also grew to become a major weapon in the arsenal of employers as they opposed unions and strikes. Hayes, thus, ended an era when federal force had protected the rights of African Americans, and he helped to initiate an era when federal and state forces protected companies against labor organizations.

That, however, was not Hayes's intent—he had genuinely been concerned about protecting federal property and public order, and had denied Scott's request for troops to smash the union. A decade later, in retirement, Hayes worried that the nation had become "a government of corporations, by corporations, and for corporations."

During the Hayes administration, the Treasury implemented two important new federal currency policies, one of which Hayes supported and other of which he opposed. His term in the White House coincided with the peak congressional strength of the Greenback party. Hayes had no sympathy for the Greenbackers or their goal of currency inflation. He believed in "hard money" or "sound money"—a currency based on precious metal rather than fiat money. Most hard-money advocates, including Hayes, also preferred a gold standard.

Hayes inherited responsibility for implementing the Resumption Act, passed in 1875, which specified that, after 1879, greenbacks could be redeemed in gold. The Resumption Act was intended, in part, to resolve the confused currency situation. When the Treasury first issued greenbacks, in 1862, they could not be exchanged for gold. At the same time, gold coins and gold certificates (much easier to carry) also circulated. As a result, there developed essentially two separate currencies, the greenback dollar and the gold dollar, with different values and purchasing powers. The postwar deflation brought the value of the two types of dollars closer together, making easier the exchange of greenbacks for gold, called resumption of specie payments. The Resumption Act necessarily linked greenbacks to the gold supply, thereby limiting their number and blocking efforts to expand the money supply by issuing more greenbacks. In 1877, inflationists focused their attention on the House of Representatives, hoping to repeal the Resumption Act. Its repeal would have meant that greenbacks remained fiat money, their volume dependent not on the gold supply but on the political process. The Democratic-controlled House did pass a repeal measure, but it died in the Republican-controlled Senate and resumption proceeded on schedule.

With resumption, some inflationists turned from a call for greenbacks to one for silver. Since 1873, as a result of a revision of the laws governing the Treasury Department, the Mint had made only gold dollars. Richard Bland, a Democratic congressman from Missouri whose labors for silver coinage earned him the nickname "Silver Dick," introduced a bill for silver coinage.[3] Given the market value of silver relative to gold and given the amount of silver specified to make a dollar under the Bland bill, the measure would have attracted nearly all silver to the Mint, thus inflating the circulating currency. Bland's bill sailed through the House with little opposition, with voting on the measure more regional than partisan, uniting the South, Midwest, and West against the Northeast. After the bill passed the House and before Senate action, Hayes announced himself opposed because it would cause inflation and drive gold out of the country.[4] That, in turn, would put the nation at

---

3 Various terms were used to describe silver coinage, including "free silver," "free and unlimited coinage of silver and gold," "free and unlimited coinage of silver and gold at a ratio of 16 to 1," or simply "silver," or even just "16 to 1." This text uses "silver coinage," except when quoting or directly paraphrasing someone. Whatever the term used, free and unlimited coinage of silver and gold at a ratio of 16 to 1 meant the Mint would not charge to make bullion into coins (it was to be "free"), that the Mint would accept and coin all silver and gold bullion presented to it (it was to be "unlimited"), and that the amount of silver in a silver dollar would weigh 16 times as much as the amount of gold in a gold dollar (it was to be "at a ratio of 16 to 1").

4 Gresham's Law, an economic theorem, states that if a nation uses coins of two different metals with a fixed rate of exchange between them, the cheaper will drive the more valuable out of circulation. During the early nineteenth century, the nation set fixed weights of metal for both gold and silver dollars, with the silver dollar about 15–16 times as heavy as the gold dollar. This initially reflected the approximate difference in the market values of the two metals. As market values changed, however, the official ratio did not, and the more valuable metal (silver, in the pre–Civil War era) disappeared from circulation. Thus, at one level, the 1873 law eliminating the silver dollar from the list of authorized coins simply recognized the reality that no silver dollars existed. At another level, however, the 1873 law was also intended, at least by some of its proponents, to put the nation on an ad hoc gold standard. Hayes was concerned that, because silver was less valuable on the market than the Bland Act specified in the ratio it set between silver and gold, Gresham's Law meant that the nation was likely to move to a de facto silver standard.

a significant disadvantage in international markets for goods and capital.

The bill passed in the Senate, sponsored by Senator William Allison, a Republican from Iowa, and with a similar regional and party division to that in the House. Hayes now faced a double dilemma: he thought the amended bill was dangerous, but the vote in favor could easily override a veto; moreover, a significant faction within the Republican party drew upon their Whig antecedents to argue that a president should use the veto only if a bill were unconstitutional or defective, and should never use the veto because of disagreement with Congress over a policy issue. However, after an extended cabinet discussion of the policy issue, related political issues, the likelihood of an override, and the proper role of the veto in policy making, Hayes went ahead and vetoed the bill, thus asserting the role of the president to block legislation he deemed unwise. His action represented a small step away from the weak presidency that had emerged during Reconstruction and a step toward a more active presidential role in policy making. Congress quickly passed the act over the veto, as most expected, with the vote nearly identical to the original vote on the measure. In his final message to Congress, Hayes called for its repeal, but no one paid much attention. In the end, the Bland-Allison Act was a bipartisan compromise that gave something to the inflationists without resorting to fiat money and without leaving the gold standard.

Hayes had promised to serve only one term. And he probably could not have secured a second nomination had he sought one. His handling of patronage had alienated significant elements in his own party, and he had estranged others by not seeking a full-scale reform of the civil service. His veto of the Bland-Allison bill had lost him still other support. Democrats continued to carp on the legitimacy of his election. His wife, Lucy Webb Hayes, the first college-educated First Lady and a committed reformer, came in for her share of criticism when the White House stopped serving alcohol and newspapers labelled her "Lemonade Lucy." It was, in fact, his decision rather than hers. Thus, in mid-1880, when a friend remarked that Hayes would "soon be out of it," he responded, "Yes, out of a scrape, out of a scrape."

Garfield and Arthur: The Deadlock Continues, 1880–1884

The 1880 election found the Republicans badly divided. Led by Conkling and Cameron, a group calling themselves the Stalwarts tried to nominate former President Grant for a third term. Blaine also sought the nomination, but the Stalwarts dismissed him and his supporters as "Half-Breeds"—not real Republicans. John Sherman, Hayes's Secretary of the Treasury, was a candidate, but he could not compete with Grant and Blaine in attracting delegates. The deadlocked convention went through thirty-six ballots before finally settling on James A. Garfield, a congressman from Ohio. Born in a log cabin, Garfield grew up in poverty, became a minister, college president, and lawyer before the Civil War, then became the Union's youngest major general. In choosing its nominee for vice-president, the convention sought both to placate the Stalwarts and to secure New York's electoral votes by nominating Conkling's chief lieutenant, Chester A. Arthur, whom Hayes had removed as head of the New York Customhouse.

The Democrats nominated Winfield Scott Hancock, another former Civil War general, but one with very little political experience. In a major gaffe, he revealed little understanding of his party's position on the tariff when he casually mentioned to a reporter that "the tariff question is a local question." Though his comment may well have been an accurate assessment of the way that Republicans usually logrolled tariff protection, it stood in direct contradiction to his party's platform that called for a tariff for revenue only.

Hancock's blunder was unusual, for both candidates worked at avoiding matters of substance during the campaign. Democrats focused on Garfield's minor role in the Crédit Mobilier scandal. Late in the campaign, they also charged that Garfield disagreed with both parties' promises to limit Chinese immigration. Garfield denied the charge, but it probably cost him the electoral votes of California and Nevada. Republicans played on Hancock's lack of political experience by publishing a book entitled *Record of the Statesmanship and Achievements of General Winfield Scott Hancock*, which was filled with blank pages. Some charged that

Hancock's wife, Elizabeth Hoxworth Hancock, a Catholic, would turn the White House over to priests if she became First Lady. The Greenbackers nominated James Weaver, yet another former Civil War general, but they attracted few votes. Garfield won the popular vote by the narrowest of margins—half a percentage point—but he won the electoral vote convincingly without carrying a single southern state, thus demonstrating that the Republicans could survive without the southern black vote.

Garfield brought to the White House a tendency to study all questions carefully. To some, this appeared indecisive. John Sherman felt that Garfield "easily changed his mind" and "veered from one impulse to another." The president accepted Sherman's advice to compromise on one major issue—alcohol returned to the White House, but Garfield took none for himself. Garfield especially despaired over the throngs who descended on Washington seeking patronage positions, confiding that he would rather run an ice-house in hell than make such decisions. He nonetheless hoped to work cooperatively with both Stalwarts and Blaine supporters. Blaine and Garfield had served together in Congress. Garfield admired Blaine's abilities and appointed him as secretary of state, the most prestigious cabinet position.

Discord soon appeared, however, between Garfield and Conkling, when Garfield refused to accept Conkling's demands regarding major appointments. Patronage was the crucially important glue for an organization such as Conkling's, and the struggle between the two men had implications for the entire political culture. As Hayes had done before him, Garfield insisted that some appointive positions were of such signal importance that they stood outside the traditional pattern whereby a president deferred to the recommendations of the senior senator from his party regarding appointments within a state. The conflict between Garfield and Conkling came to focus on the most significant patronage job in the country, the head of the New York Customhouse. Refusing to accept the argument that Conkling should specify the new customs collector because the post was in his state, Garfield thereby challenged the entire Senate, for all senators cherished the right to recommend their supporters for federal positions in their states.

But in his fight with Conkling, Garfield showed himself to be politically shrewd, for he withdrew all other appointments from Senate action until after the Senate acted on his choice for collector—thereby holding all other appointments hostage to the vote of senators on his choice for collector. His supporters, especially John Sherman, and Garfield himself wheedled and bargained with senators in a way that no president had done for many years. When Conkling signaled his defeat by resigning his Senate seat, Garfield scored an important victory for presidential control over appointments.

On July 2, 1881, four months after taking the oath of office, Garfield was shot while walking through a Washington railroad station. His assassin, Charles Guiteau, a mentally unstable religious fanatic, called himself "a Stalwart of the Stalwarts" and claimed he had acted to save the Republican party. With Garfield's death, Vice-President Arthur became president. Candidates for vice-president were typically chosen for their ability to add regional or political balance to the ticket, and rarely for their ability to serve as president. This was especially true of Arthur, whom Garfield had picked to help carry New York and, simultaneously, to mollify Conkling. Nonetheless Arthur moved to the White House.

A Stalwart and long-time close ally of Conkling, Arthur was probably best known, beyond his Stalwart connections, as an honest and capable administrator and a dapper dresser. He had held one of the highest paying posts in the civil service and had invested his earnings wisely. His predecessors in the White House had moved tables around to cover threadbare carpets because Congress refused the funds for anything new, but Arthur dug into his own pocket and lavishly redecorated. His abstemious midwestern predecessors had fretted over serving wine in the White House, but Arthur's state dinners featured as many as eight varieties of wine to accompany as many courses of French cuisine.

In his administrative decisions, Arthur proved that, as one of his former New York associates said, "He isn't 'Chet' Arthur any more; he's the President." He somewhat favored Stalwarts in his handling of patronage, but not to their satisfaction—one complained that "He has done less for us than Garfield, or even Hayes."

Arthur maintained Garfield's appointments that had so antagonized Conkling, continued an investigation into corruption in the
Post Office even though Stalwarts were implicated, and suggested
further reform of the spoils system. During his first year in office,
he could count on a Republican majority in the House of Representatives. The Senate, however, was tied between the two parties
and often stood at the center of Republican factional feuding. After the 1882 elections, Arthur faced a Democratic majority in the
House. Nonetheless, during Arthur's presidency, Congress made
the first major revisions in the tariff since 1875 and also developed and passed two important new policies—the Chinese Exclusion Act of 1882 and the Pendleton Act reforming the civil service
in 1883.

By early 1882, a steady increase in imports meant that the tariff was feeding a rapidly swelling federal budget surplus: $66 mil-
lion in 1880, $100 million in 1881, and nearly $146 million in
1882. (See Table 2.4.) Mugwumps joined many Democrats in demanding lower tariffs, pointing to the budget surplus and claiming
that lower tariffs would stimulate the economy more than protection. Arthur, in early 1882, asked Congress to set up a commission
to study the tariff, and Congress did so. Though dominated by protectionists, the commission called for reductions in import duties.

Democratic gains in the 1882 congressional elections prompted
Republican congressmen in the lame-duck session to undertake tariff revision while they still controlled both houses of Congress.
Working quickly, the Senate approved some substantial reductions. Only one Republican voted against, but ten Democrats supported the measure. Republican protectionists in the House, however, produced a measure that changed the rates on certain goods
considerably but altered overall duties only slightly and bore little
resemblance to either the commission's recommendations or the
Senate's bill. The Senate nonetheless approved the House version
of the bill by a near-straight party vote. The House also divided
largely along party lines, with 19 Democrats joining the Republicans in favor and 12 Republicans voting with the Democrats. Most
of the Democrats in favor considered protection a necessity in
seeking reelection in manufacturing areas, and most of the Repub-

licans who were opposed found the rates too low. In rejecting the work of the tariff commission, congressional Republicans made it clear that they intended to keep control over the process of distributing tariff benefits to their constituents. Arthur signed what had come to be called the Mongrel Tariff.

Both of the major new policies approved by Arthur commanded significant support across party lines. In the case of the Chinese Exclusion Act of 1882, the Republican, Democratic, and Greenback platforms of 1880 had all called for limits on Chinese immigration. Some 300,000 Chinese immigrants had entered the United States since the late 1840s, when the California Gold Rush drew prospectors from many parts of the world. By 1870, Chinese immigrants accounted for half of all miners in California and were also prominent in the ranks of railroad construction crews and agricultural hands. The 1880 census counted some 100,000 Chinese immigrants in the United States, 80 percent of them in the West.

Almost from the beginning, Chinese immigrants had encountered discrimination and violence. A major anti-Chinese riot broke out in Los Angeles in 1871. When the depression of the 1870s set in, white workers blamed Chinese immigrants for driving down wages and causing unemployment. Anti-Chinese riots flared in San Francisco in 1877 and elsewhere thereafter. In these riots, the cry of white demonstrators was usually the same: "The Chinese Must Go." This slogan came out of agitation in San Francisco in 1877, when the Workingmen's Party of California gained a significant following by blaming high unemployment and low wages on Chinese workers and the great capitalists who hired them. Nearly everyone, therefore, understood the parties' demands for Chinese exclusion as gestures aimed at placating white workers, especially on the Pacific Coast. In 1882, influenced by their western assemblies, the Knights of Labor also adopted a strongly anti-Chinese stance.

Hayes had vetoed a bill restricting Chinese immigration in 1879, but in 1880 his administration negotiated a treaty with China that permitted the United States to "regulate, limit, or suspend" the immigration of Chinese laborers. In 1882, Senator John Miller, a California Republican, introduced a bill to bar Chinese immigration for twenty years and to prohibit Chinese already in the country from becoming naturalized citizens.[5] Miller's bill drew strong support from westerners, mostly Republicans, and from white-supremacist southern Democrats. It passed both houses of Congress easily, drawing nearly unanimous support from Democrats and western Republicans against opposition from northeastern Republicans, especially veterans of the abolition movement.

Arthur vetoed Miller's bill, arguing that it violated the treaty of 1880 and that twenty years was too long for such a blanket exclusion on immigration. He also suggested that the bill might limit access to potentially lucrative Asian markets and "drive their trade and commerce into more friendly hands." In response, Congress revised the bill, cut the period of exclusion to ten years, and added a statement that the bill did not violate the 1880 treaty. Thus modified, it drew even more votes, and Arthur signed it. The Chinese Exclusion Act of 1882 prohibited entry to all Chinese except teachers, students, merchants, tourists, and officials and barred naturalization of Chinese immigrants. It marked the first time in American history that Congress had set limits on immigration. The pattern of blaming immigrants—whether from China or elsewhere—for national economic problems was to continue and expand, however, as was the pattern of looking for federal legislation to limit immigration or restrain immigrants.

The other major new policy of Arthur's administration was a change in the rules governing the civil service, intended to change it from a system based solely on patronage to one in which some appointments were to be based on merit. The bill was sponsored by Senator George Pendleton, a Democrat from Ohio. Pendleton had first proposed a civil service reform measure in 1880, and he reintroduced it in 1881 on the same day that Arthur sent Congress a message calling for civil service reform. While some members

---

5 Chinese immigrants, by most interpretations, had been barred from naturalization by act of Congress in 1790 which limited naturalized citizenship to "free, white persons." In 1870, this was amended to permit persons of African descent to become naturalized citizens. Nonetheless, local courts had applied the law differently in different areas, permitting a small number of Chinese immigrants to become naturalized citizens.

of both parties genuinely supported the idea of awarding governmental jobs based on a merit system, because of distaste for the spoils system or a commitment to the principles of expertise and continuity that were central to the merit system, larger numbers in both parties saw partisan advantage in supporting such reform. The Democrats, in promoting Pendleton's bill, hoped to gain support from Mugwumps and others who blamed the spoils system for corruption and who asserted that Garfield's assassin had been a disappointed office-seeker. At the same time, the Democrats anticipated a direct political advantage from reducing the ability of Republicans to assess federal workers (whom they had placed) for campaign funds.

After Democrats swept many of the 1882 congressional elections and seemed poised to win the presidency in 1884, many Republicans joined the supporters of civil service reform, both to appeal to reformers and to protect their appointees from removal should a Democrat indeed win in 1884. (The law was worded to prevent removal for partisan reasons of those holding jobs designated to be filled through the merit system, even if they were themselves appointed through the patronage system.) When Republicans in the 1883 lame-duck session took up the Pendleton bill with enthusiasm, Democrats dragged their feet, one of them calling it "a bill to perpetuate in office the Republicans who now control the patronage of the Government." In the end, nearly all Republicans favored it, and the Democrats divided.

As finally approved, the Pendleton Act removed certain governmental positions from the patronage system, designated them as *classified*, and specified that in the future they were to be filled through a system of competitive examinations. The law also created a five-person civil service commission to supervise the new system. Initially only 15 percent of federal positions were classified, but the law authorized the president to add positions to the classified list. The person who held an office when it was first placed on the classified list was protected from removal for partisan reasons, so presidents used the law to protect their own appointees from removal by their successor. When those appointees retired, however, their replacements came through competitive examinations. In this way, the law used patronage in the short run to bring about the demise of the patronage system over the long run. By 1901, the law applied to 44 percent of federal employees, and most state and local governments slowly came to follow a similar approach.

Cleveland: The Deadlock Lengthens, 1884–1888

In the end, Arthur proved a more fitting president than anyone might have predicted. In 1882, however, he had learned that he had Bright's disease, a fatal kidney condition. He concealed the disease from all but his closest family and friends. Given his failing health, he made little serious effort to win his party's nomination in 1884. Had he been in full health, he would have faced great difficulty in getting nominated, given the way he had alienated Stalwarts without dispelling the mistrust of reformers.

The 1884 campaign pitted James G. Blaine, one of the Republicans' most experienced and capable leaders, against a Democratic political novice, Grover Cleveland. Blaine had left the cabinet shortly after Garfield's death and prepared his memoirs. They constituted two hefty volumes and appeared, probably not coincidentally, in the same year he finally won his party's presidential nomination. His running mate was John Logan of Illinois. Tilden could have had the Democratic nomination but refused to seek it. The Democrats then turned to someone who had just proven he could carry New York state: Grover Cleveland, who had moved quickly from election as mayor of Buffalo, New York, in 1881 to election as governor of New York in 1882, when he benefited from a serious rift in the state GOP. Called "Uncle Jumbo" by his nephews, Cleveland quickly emerged as a political heavyweight too, earning a reputation for integrity and political courage. Though he had little in the way of experience or record of accomplishment, that was no serious impediment to his nomination because the Democrats were most interested in his proven ability to carry New York.

The 1884 presidential contest held the potential for an unusual amount of party-line-crossing, for Blaine's Irish ancestry appealed to the Irish voters who made up the core of New York City's Democratic organization. On the other hand, many Mugwumps distrusted Blaine and liked Cleveland's reputation for principled firmness. The campaign quickly turned nasty, as both sides tried to demonstrate the other candidate's personal shortcomings. To embarrass Blaine, Mugwumps revealed a letter he had written years before, in which he asked the recipient to "burn this letter." Throughout the campaign, parades of Democrats tramped through city streets shouting "Burn this letter!" and periodically lighting up sheets of stationery. Blaine supporters gleefully trumpeted the fact that Cleveland, never married, had fathered a child a decade before, and Republican campaigners set up a cry of "Ma! Ma! Where's my pa?" In the end, the scandals probably balanced each other. They may even have unified the parties and concealed their internal divisions better than a serious, issue-oriented campaign. In addition, Republicans subsidized the campaign of Benjamin Butler, the Greenback Labor candidate, in the expectation that he would draw working-class votes from the Democrats in urban areas. He did poorly in the cities, however, and probably drew some votes from Blaine in rural parts of the Midwest.

As with all the elections from 1876 through 1888, the outcome of 1884's contest hinged on the electoral votes of New York state. Blaine had hoped to cut into New Your City's large and traditionally Democratic Irish vote. A few days before the election, however, at a political meeting in New York City, Blaine heard an obscure preacher refer to the Democrats as the party of "rum, Romanism [an insulting reference to Catholicism], and rebellion." Instead of quickly disavowing the slight to his Irish Catholic supporters, Blaine ignored the phrase until newspapers blasted it the next day. In the absence of public opinion polls, the impact can only be guessed: one prominent Catholic thought that it cost Blaine as many as 50,000 votes, but others, then and since, have disputed whether it cost the Republican any significant number. As the Democrats had hoped, Cleveland carried New York state, but he did so by fewer than 1,200 votes out of more than 1 million cast. Cleveland's victory resulted from many factors, including Conkling's refusal to rally the remnants of his organization in support of his old enemy Blaine and the strong campaign of the Prohibitionists, who won 25,000 votes in New York state, most of them taken from the Republican column.

When Cleveland moved into the White House, he became the first Democrat to do so since the departure of James Buchanan twenty-four years before—before the Civil War, emancipation, and Reconstruction; before the development of a national railroad and telegraph network; before widespread industrialization, the emergence of big business, massive immigration from Europe, the burgeoning of the cities, and the economic development of much of the West. Republicans were directly responsible for some of those changes, claimed credit for others, and had long argued that a Democratic administration would try to turn back the clock. Cleveland, however, was no Bourbon reactionary. He revered the Constitution, including the Fourteenth and Fifteenth amendments. In his inaugural address, which he recited from memory—the only president ever to do so—he pledged "equal and exact justice to all men" and promised to protect the rights of African Americans. To the surprise of many, he even appointed a few blacks to federal positions, though not in the South.

Though not interested in turning back the clock, Cleveland heartily subscribed to the Jacksonian principles of his party and took a highly restricted view of the role of the federal government. Government, he thought, ought to stay out of citizens' lives as much as possible. Like Jackson, he defined the proper role of the president as to restrain Congress from granting privileges to some at the expense of others. He classed railroad land grants and the protective tariff as forms of favoritism, by which government improperly benefited particular individuals or companies. He fretted over the growth of federal authority and hoped to restore a better balance between federal and state power.

Of those who applauded Cleveland's inauguration, Mugwumps probably held the most unrealistic expectations. Some Mugwumps had dubbed him "Grover the Good" and many of them expected him to dismantle the spoils system. Cleveland alienated some Democrats when he refused to give them positions they wanted, but he did not dismantle the patronage system. He did insist on demonstrated ability as well as party loyalty in his appointees, and he advised federal appointees to avoid partisan politics. During his administration, he named Democrats to replace three-quarters of the non-classified federal officeholders, nearly all of them Republicans. He also increased by more than two-thirds the number of classified positions, thereby extending the merit system even as he protected his own appointees from removal.

Republicans held onto a majority in the Senate and cited the Tenure in Office Act as a constraint on Cleveland's ability to remove Republicans from appointive positions. Originally passed to prevent Andrew Johnson from removing officials aligned with the Radical Republicans, the law, as amended in 1869, reserved for the Senate a significant role in the removal of officials whom the Senate had confirmed. Senate Republicans served notice on Cleveland that they expected full documentation on any removals and intended to investigate removals they considered improper. Considering this a violation of the president's constitutional authority, Cleveland refused to comply and sent a strong message to the Senate explaining his reasons. Despite some bristling, the Senate backed down and eventually repealed the Tenure in Office Act, marking another step toward a strengthened presidency.

Like Jackson, Cleveland asserted the power of the presidency through the veto. He established his record number of vetoes mostly by giving close attention to bills that he considered shameless raids on the federal treasury. Since the Civil War, Republicans had been generous to Union veterans who sought pensions for service-related disabilities. Most veterans applied through the federal Pension Bureau, which investigated to confirm that a disability was war-related and, if so, specified a pension amount based on the extent of the disability. Cleveland tried to make the Pension Bureau more efficient, but concentrated especially on pensions granted through a private bill, an act of Congress that applied only to a specific person.

Private bills were usually logrolled with no investigation or debate, as members approved the bills of others and expected approval of theirs in turn. The volume of such measures grew steadily. During 1885–1887, they accounted for two-fifths of all bills passed by the House and more than half of all approved by the Senate. Cleveland carefully studied all the private pension bills he received—2,099 over four years—and vetoed 228 of them, thus drawing the wrath of both the sponsors of the vetoed bills and the GAR, which acted as a powerful lobby for veterans. In 1887, he also vetoed a proposal to provide pensions to all disabled Union veterans. Such a proposal, Cleveland argued, would create a vast, expensive, and often fraudulent system of charity. That same year, he further antagonized the GAR when he agreed with a routine recommendation by R. C. Drum, the adjutant-general (and a Republican), to clear out some Washington attics by returning to the southern states the Confederate battle flags that Union forces had captured during the Civil War. GAR leaders, followed closely by many Republican politicians and newspapers, condemned the order as an outrage and an insult to the memory of the Union soldiers who gave their lives to take those flags. Cleveland rescinded the order.

Cleveland's skirmishes with Congress, especially those with the Republican Senate, confirmed the partisan deadlock that began in 1874 and differed but little from squabbles between his Republican predecessors and the Democratic majorities they had faced in the House. As was true of the Bland-Allison Act, Chinese exclusion, and the Pendleton Act, the most important new policies during Cleveland's first administration—the Interstate Commerce Act and the Dawes Severalty Act—both originated in Congress rather than in the White House and both were broadly bipartisan in their origin and support.

The Interstate Commerce Act grew out of political pressure from a variety of sources, having in common a commitment to a more prominent federal role regarding the railroads. Those calling for government action, however, disagreed among themselves in defining that role. Since then, historians have also disagreed in their analyses of which groups had the most influence on the law's final provisions. At issue were a number of railroad practices. Railroads charged lower freight rates to shippers sending goods a long distance ("long haul" rates) than those they charged to shippers sending goods a short distance ("short haul" rates), on the grounds that it was less expensive per mile to send freight over a long distance. Rebates were refunds, usually paid to shippers who did a great amount of business with a railroad. Rebates were sometimes given in appreciation for the shipper's business, but other times they were demanded by a large shipper (Standard Oil was notorious for this practice) as the price of their selection of one railroad over a competing line. Rebates and the long- short-haul rate differential are both examples of rate discrimination—charging different prices to different shippers. Pooling was a practice whereby several railroads operating through the same region agreed among themselves to divide up the business and to set similar prices rather than compete with each other and, perhaps, cut prices. One of the most famous, the "Iowa Pool," consisted of railroads operating between Chicago and Omaha, across Iowa; it began in 1870 and continued for more than a decade, although it lost some of its effectiveness after 1874.

The first state railroad commission dated back to 1832, and the first state law aimed at preventing rate discrimination came in 1844. By the 1860s, merchants in several states were agitating against rate discrimination and were joined in the early 1870s by independent oil companies facing competitive pressures from Standard Oil. Farm organizations and granger parties took the lead in securing laws regulating railroad rates in several midwestern states, beginning with Illinois in 1871. In 1877, the Supreme Court upheld such rate-setting in *Munn* v. *Illinois*. A subsequent Supreme Court decision in 1886, however, involving the Wabash railroad, banned states from regulating railroad rates that involved interstate commerce. After the decline of the Grange in the late 1870s, merchants again became the most prominent advocates of regulation. By the early 1880s, even some railroad officials joined in an effort to stop the vicious rate competition taking place in some areas.

Eventually the pressures for governmental action regarding railroad rates came to focus on Congress. The House first considered the issue in 1876, at the urging of independent oil companies in Pennsylvania. In 1878, Congressman John Reagan, a Democrat from Texas, pushed through the House a bill that prohibited rate

discrimination and pooling, but it died in the Senate. Reagan expanded and reintroduced his bill in subsequent sessions. One version passed the House in late 1885. Eventually Senator Shelby
Cullom, Republican of Illinois, introduced a more moderate bill,
which took a more flexible view of long- short-haul differentials,
ignored pooling, and left enforcement to a commission rather than
to the courts. Neither bill provided for regulation of rates. The
Senate approved the Cullom bill in early 1886. The Wabash decision of the Supreme Court, later in 1886, which prohibited states
from regulating railroads engaged in interstate commerce, may
have provided the catalyst for final action, for the two houses compromised between the Reagan and Cullom bills in early 1887,
passing the Interstate Commerce Act. The final count in the Senate
found 50 in favor and 20 against. Of the opponents, fifteen were
Republicans, most came from the Northeast, and five had once
served as presidents of railroad companies. Similar patterns pre-
vailed in the House, although there some of the votes against came
from those who preferred the more stringent Reagan bill. Midwestern Republicans and southern Democrats made up the two
largest blocs of votes in favor. Cleveland studied the bill carefully,
then signed.

The Interstate Commerce Act created the Interstate Commerce Commission (ICC). Its five members were to serve six-year
terms and no more than three of them could be from the same
party. The law prohibited pools and rebates, directed railroads to
eliminate some differential rates for short and long hauls, and
specified that rates should be "reasonable and just." It did not give
the ICC power to set rates or to punish companies whose rates violated the law's provisions. When the ICC did try to impose rates,
the Supreme Court stopped it.

The legislative process for passing the railroad regulatory
measure proved different from that to which most Congressmen
were accustomed. Unlike tariff rate-setting, in which most Congressmen dutifully sought to protect what they perceived to be
their constituents' interests and built a majority through logrolling,
regulatory legislation involved economic interests in conflict with
each other—satisfying farmers and merchants, for example, meant

alienating railroads. Thus, where distributive legislation could often be easily decided through logrolling, regulatory legislation has
typically required compromise. In the end, the Interstate Commerce Act drew opposition not only from railroad companies,
which concluded that it allowed too much governmental regulation, but also from some farm groups, which thought it did not
mandate enough. This struggle over the creation of the ICC fore-
shadowed important aspects of twentieth-century law making—
competing interest groups asking Congress for action, and Congress mediating among those disparate interests to create national
policy.

The other major policy change of the Cleveland administration, the Dawes Severalty Act, officially known as the Indian
Emancipation Act, marked less a change of direction than a culmination of changes in federal Indian policy. Leading scholars, notably Lewis Henry Morgan of the Smithsonian Institution in his
widely acclaimed *Ancient Society* (1877), had introduced an evolutionary concept of culture. Rather than seeing each culture as
unique, as most twentieth-century anthropologists have done,
Morgan and his followers considered all people to stand at different stages in an evolutionary process that ranged from "savagery"
through "barbarism" to "civilization." All people, they argued,
tended naturally to develop toward higher cultural types. The
highest level of civilization, most white Americans agreed, had developed among the people of western Europe and people of European descent now living in other parts of the world. Based upon
this understanding of culture and civilization, federal policy makers defined American Indians as barbarians and sought to accelerate the evolutionary process: to "civilize" the Indians, which meant
making them like their white contemporaries.

Education formed an important element in this government-
induced transformation. In boarding schools, some set up on reservations and a few in far-off eastern cities, teachers prohibited Indian children from speaking their own language, practicing their
religion, and otherwise exercising their own culture. The teachers
hoped that this would make it easier to impose white cultural patterns upon their charges. Other programs sought to train adult In-

dian men as farmers or mechanics. Indian Affairs officials also prohibited American Indians from holding a number of religious ceremonies that the former considered barbaric, notably the Sun Dance of the Plains tribes and the Snake Dance and Katchina ceremony of the Southwest tribes.

Grant's Peace Policy had included guarantees to the Indians of reservation lands along with educational programs. As more and more white railroaders, cattlemen, miners, and homesteaders moved into the West, however, they increasingly challenged the reservation policy—railroads wanted to build across reservation lands, miners wanted to prospect on them, farmers and ranchers coveted them for agriculture. At the same time, Congress balked at allocating the full amount of funds needed to form a decent educational system for American Indians. The Republican party itself split on the issue, between a northeastern and midwestern group that favored the continuation of special protections for Indians, including reservations and federally sponsored education, and a western wing that opposed most such programs. Southern Democrats increasingly sided with the westerners. Nonetheless, by 1887 a compromise seemed to be possible, one that would satisfy both the westerners eager to open up some reservation lands and the humanitarian reformers interested in protecting Indian rights and in fostering assimilation. The compromise became known as the severalty policy.

Sponsored by Henry G. Dawes, a Republican senator from Massachusetts, the severalty bill was widely considered a significant step, perhaps the most significant single step, toward final assimilation of the American Indians. It committed the government to severalty, that is, a policy to end the reservation system under which Indian people held land in common and instead to divide the land into individual family holdings. Once reservation lands were divided up, the government was then to sell the remaining land—perhaps two-thirds of the total—and hold the proceeds from the land sales in trust to finance Indian education and related programs. Allotment, therefore, gained support both from those who wanted to protect and educate the Indians and from those who wanted to get Indian lands on the market.

The bill drew wide support from most who had defended the Indians in the past. It was widely seen as simply the proper culmination of the assimilation campaign, for it had, as its ultimate object, making the Indians into self-sufficient, property-conscious, profit-oriented, individual farmers—the model citizen of nineteenth-century white America. Starkly revealing the evolutionary view of civilization ("progress") that most genteel reformers shared, as well as the virtues that most Americans ascribed to private property, Dawes put it this way at a conference in 1885:

[When land is held in common,] there is no enterprise to make your home any better than that of your neighbor. There is no selfishness, which is at the bottom of civilization. Till this people will consent to give up their lands, and divide them among their citizens so that each can own the land he cultivates, they will not make much more progress.

Individual land ownership and acquisitiveness, however, ran directly contrary to Indian cultural patterns that had always emphasized that land was for the use of all, and that sharing it was a primary obligation of all people.

Some Indian leaders supported the measure, but others urged Congress not to pass it. Delegates from the Cherokee, Creek, and Choctaw nations, for example, petitioned Congress to oppose Dawes's bill. "Our people have not asked for or authorized this," they stressed in their petition, explaining that, "Our own laws regulate a system of land tenure suited to our condition." No other participants in the debate argued in favor of continuing the reservation system and the communal ownership of land as a way to protect and foster Indian cultures. In the minds of the reformers, fostering Indian cultures was equivalent to condemning Indians to a permanent status of barbarism and to denying them the "blessings of civilization."

Congress approved the Dawes Act despite the protests of Indian representatives. The result of allotment bore out the insightful warning of Senator Henry Teller, Republican from Colorado, one of the few white opponents of the Dawes Bill, who called it "a bill to despoil the Indians of their land and to make them vagabonds on the face of the earth." Despite safeguards, through implementation of the new policy, Indians sometimes received land allotments before they were prepared to take them, sometimes even though they did not want them, and many quickly lost their holdings through fraud or manipulation by land-hungry whites. Though a good deal of "surplus" land was sold, allotment did not end the reservation system nor did it reduce the Indians' dependence upon the federal government. It did separate the Indians from some of their lands, often the most valuable.

As was true of most significant legislation in the Gilded Age, Congress created the ICC and the Dawes Act with little involvement by the president. Until late 1887—less than a year before the 1888 presidential election—Cleveland did little to put a personal or a partisan stamp on his administration other than to veto pension scams and replace Republican postmasters. In 1885, he urged Congress to repeal the Bland-Allison Act, but House Democrats blocked action.

Deciding late in his administration to launch a major assault on the protective tariff, Cleveland devoted his entire annual message to Congress in December 1887 to a call for tariff reduction. He claimed that the existing tariff posed two serious dangers: it created a rapidly growing federal budget surplus and thereby tempted Congress to lavish federal funds on ill-advised pork-barrel projects, and it encouraged the growth of monopolies by eliminating meaningful competition to domestic manufacturers. Cleveland hoped to focus the 1888 presidential contest on substantive issues rather than the personal ones that had dominated the campaign of 1884, and he said privately that he chose to concentrate on the tariff because he wanted his party to "stand for something."

Cleveland's action provoked a serious division within his own party. So long as the Democrats did not have to take responsibility for the tariff, they could freely criticize Republican policies. Now, when a president of their own party asked them to take action, they failed. In keeping with his view of the proper role of the president, Cleveland exerted little leadership beyond his initial message, leaving the initiative to congressional leaders. House Democrats treated it not as a matter of party principle but as just another exercise in logrolling. On a near-straight party vote, the House passed

This cartoon, originally published in 1874, was used to demonstrate how white voting officials in the South intimidated African-American voters. It also illustrates a typical procedure for casting votes in the era before the secret ballot. Outside the polling place, voters were given a "party ticket" by party activists. They then placed the ticket in a ballot box in sight of voting officials and anyone else who cared to watch. This also illustrates one aspect of "waving the bloody shirt," in which Republican campaigners accused Democrats of subverting the democratic process in the South. *Courtesy Smithsonian Institution*

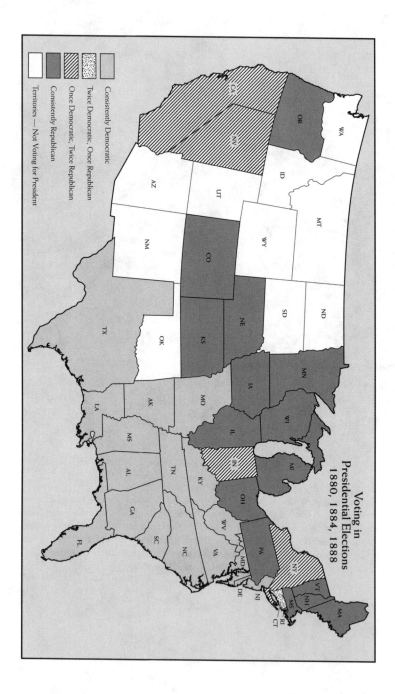

Voting in
Presidential Elections
1880, 1884, 1888

Consistently Democratic
Twice Democratic, Once Republican
Once Democratic, Twice Republican
Consistently Republican
Territories — Not Voting for President

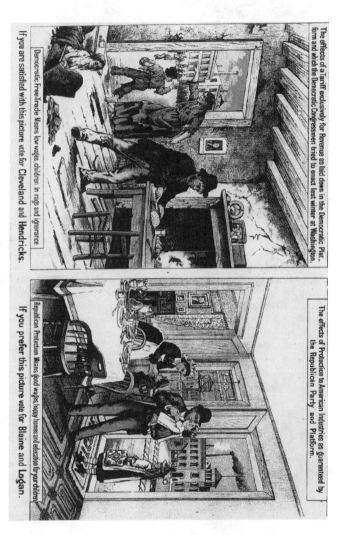

The effects of a Tariff exclusively for Revenue as laid down in the Democratic Plat-form and which the Democratic Congressmen tried to enact last winter at Washington.

Democratic Free-Trade Means low wages, children in rags and ignorance.

If you are satisfied with this picture vote for Cleveland and **Hendricks.**

The effects of Protection to American Industries as guaranteed by the Republican Party and Platform.

Republican Protection Means good wages, happy homes and education for your children!

If you prefer this picture vote for **Blaine and Logan.**

This Republican campaign poster from 1884 illustrates their use of the protective tariff to appeal to urban workers. Blaine, the Republican candidate in 1884, was especially associated with a shift in Republican campaign tactics from emphasizing the bloody shirt to emphasizing the tariff. *Courtesy Smithsonian Institution*

In this cartoon from the 1870s, the Grange, in the symbolic form of a farmer, tries to awaken Americans to the imminent danger they face. The danger is symbolically represented as a train (railroads were the largest and most powerful of the new industrial corporations), and its cars are labeled for the economic and political dangers that grangers associated with the rapid transformation of the economy: consolidation (mergers that created large and powerful corporations), extortion (financial gain through intimidation), bribery (corruption of the political process), usurpation (loss of rights), and depression. The citizens, however, are oblivious to the danger. One is reading a newspaper labeled *The Partisan*, suggesting that commitment to the major parties compounded the danger Americans faced. *Courtesy Culver Pictures*

Mary Elizabeth Clyens Lease was one of the best known and most effective campaigners for the Populist party in the early 1890s. After reading law and gaining admission to the bar, she turned to political organizing in 1888. She took part in the founding of the Kansas Populist party and was catapulted to national fame by her speeches in 1890. Called "Mary 'Yellin' Lease" by her opponents, she is attributed with originating the slogan, "Raise less corn and more hell!" She refused to support William Jennings Bryan in 1896 and took little prominent role in politics thereafter. *Courtesy Kansas State Historical Society*

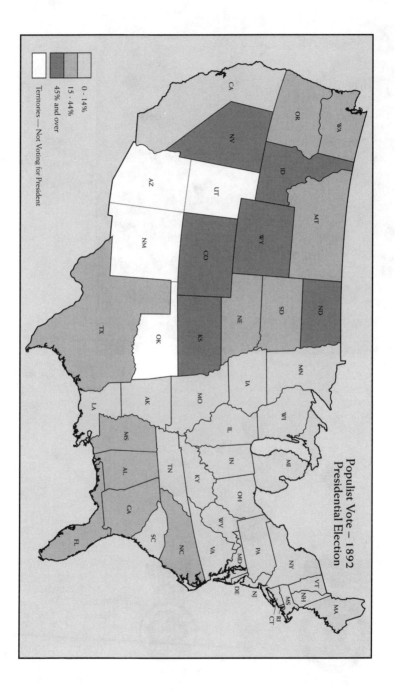

Populist Vote – 1892
Presidential Election

0 - 14%
15 - 44%
45% and over
Territories — Not Voting for President

Opposite top: William Jennings Bryan took his presidential campaign directly to the voters in 1896, focusing especially in the Midwest. Usually accompanied by his wife, Mary Baird Bryan, he traveled 18,000 miles by train, and he spoke, at least briefly, nearly every time his train stopped. *Courtesy Nebraska State Historical Society*

Opposite bottom: The 1896 presidential campaign saw the first use of the campaign button with a built-in pin on the back. All these buttons are in support of Bryan and silver. The "16 to 1" was short for Bryan's call for the free and unlimited coinage of gold and silver at a ratio of 16 to 1, the ratio between the weight of silver in a silver dollar and the weight of gold in a gold dollar. The Bryan campaign featured many clever depictions of 16:1, including clock faces showing 16 minutes to 1. He was sometimes met at train stations by 16 young people dressed in white and 1 dressed in yellow. *Courtesy Nebraska State Historical Society*

Above: William McKinley stayed at home in 1896 and campaigned for the presidency from his front porch. The Republican campaign, headed by McKinley's friend Marcus A. Hanna, brought trainloads of voters to hear McKinley. McKinley's visitors—numbering in the thousands by the end of the campaign—destroyed nearly all the plants in his lawn and whittled out hundreds of souvenir splinters from his famous porch. *Courtesy Ohio Historical Society*

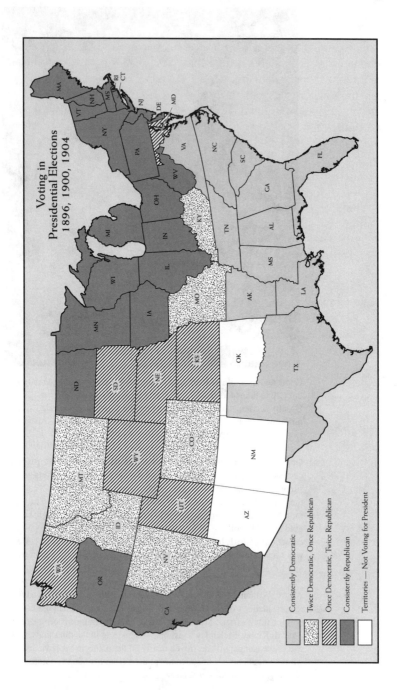

Voting in
Presidential Elections
1896, 1900, 1904

Consistently Democratic

Twice Democratic, Once Republican

Once Democratic, Twice Republican

Consistently Republican

Territories — Not Voting for President

a bill that slightly cut overall tariff rates but favored southern sugar producers. The Republican Senate responded in kind, drafting
an entirely separate bill based on their commitment to protection,
but then adjourned without voting on the result. In the end,
Cleveland's bold call for tariff reduction served only to confirm that
the parties remained deadlocked over issues that were central to
one party's self-definition.

Breaking the Deadlock?
Harrison and the Fifty-first Congress, 1888–1890

In 1888, the Democrats renominated Cleveland, but he backed off
from the tariff issue and refused to campaign actively because he
thought it below the dignity of the presidency. The Democratic
National Committee waged a lackluster campaign that failed to
give the tariff issue the prominence that Cleveland had assigned it
a few months before.

The Republicans nominated Benjamin Harrison, a former Senator from Indiana and former Civil War general whom many saw as
Blaine's political heir. A man of intelligence, ability, and integrity,
Harrison lacked personal warmth and sometimes alienated those
he dealt with face-to-face. He limited his campaigning to greeting
crowds of well-wishers who appeared at his home in Indianapolis.
Fully accepting the challenge that Cleveland had posed over the
tariff, the Republicans campaigned aggressively in defense of protection of U.S. manufactures, using it to unify their party and to
mobilize campaign workers and voters. As early as 1880, Blaine
had advocated such an approach as the strongest possible campaign tactic, one that addressed the realities of an the emerging industrial society. Under the leadership of Matthew Quay, Republican boss of Pennsylvania and head of the Republican National
Committee, they systematically approached business leaders on
the tariff issue and succeeded in raising unprecedented amounts of
campaign money—over $3 million. This method of fund-raising
marked an important change from the previous practice of assessing patronage appointees, candidates, and other party activists.
The Republicans used their new-found funds especially to mount a

campaign of education on the tariff, through publication and distribution of printed campaign materials in enormous quantities. The prominence of the tariff issue brought into politics a number of organizations not previously active, especially organizations of manufacturers. Not wholly forsaking the bloody shirt, Republicans also attacked Cleveland's vetoes of pensions for Union veterans and his (rescinded) order for the return of the Confederate battle flags, especially when addressing Union veterans.

Toward the end of the campaign, Republicans gleefully released a letter from Sir Lionel Sackville-West, the British minister to the United States. In response to a letter claiming to be from a former British subject inquiring how to vote, Sackville-West recommended Cleveland. Republican orators cited the letter and painted Cleveland as the pliant tool of British interests. Cleveland officially asked the British to recall Sackville-West, then sent him home before the British acted.

Though Harrison easily won in the electoral voting, he received fewer popular votes than Cleveland: just under 48 percent for Harrison compared to nearly 49 percent for Cleveland. Cleveland's popular plurality came on the strength of large southern majorities. He lost the most crucial states, New York and Indiana, by the narrowest of margins—a switch by one voter out of every 200 in New York and by one of every 500 in Indiana would have returned Cleveland to the White House. Though New York and Indiana were close, Democrats had lost support in some previously safe areas—Harrison came within 500 votes of carrying West Virginia and 1,600 of carrying Virginia. Some Democrats blamed Cleveland for their loss because he had handled the tariff issue so badly, and Blaine also credited the tariff issue with bringing Republican gains, especially in the border states and the South.

Cleveland's faults were only part of the Democrats' problem, however, for the Republicans had out-organized and out-spent them across the board. After the results were in, according to one oft-repeated story, Harrison dumbfounded Quay by telling him that "Providence has given us the victory." Quay later assured friends that "Providence hadn't a damned thing to do with it." Under Quay's direction, the Republicans had, in fact, buried their factional feuds, focused their campaign on protection, raised unprecedented amounts of campaign funds, and staged a thorough and methodical campaign. They not only won the presidency but also secured majorities in both the House and Senate. In 1889, for the first time since 1875, the Republicans held the potential to make significant changes in public policy.

With Harrison in the White House and majorities in both houses of Congress, Republicans made clear from the first day of the Fifty-first Congress, December 2, 1889, that they intended to do a lot and to do it quickly. Members of the House, however, had developed many tactics to delay or obstruct action. When Democrats brought the House to a halt using such time-tested measures, Speaker Thomas B. Reed calmly pulled the rug out from under them by announcing new rules. His first such ruling disposed of the "disappearing quorum," a practice whereby members of the minority refused to answer a quorum call even though present, thereby stalling House decision making. After the Democrats practiced this maneuver several times over the first few weeks of the session, Reed simply ordered the clerks to record as present all House members actually present—at which, the ostensibly absent Democrats loudly denounced him as a "czar" and "tyrant." Other new rules followed, all intended to reduce obstruction and expedite House business. With the Reed rules in place, the House gave high priority to the tariff and the federal surplus, closely linked issues that had briefly given Cleveland the initiative in his critique of protection.

The Republicans wanted to cut the budget surplus but not to reduce protection. Indeed, cutting tariff rates would not necessarily reduce the surplus (as can be seen in Table 2.4). Lower rates after 1870 apparently encouraged more imports and actually increased the surplus. Some proposed higher rates as having more potential to keep out imports and thereby reduce the surplus. Led by William McKinley of Ohio, the House Ways and Means Committee held extensive hearings on the matter. In an effort to broaden the base of voter support for protection, the bill the committee generated—known as the McKinley bill—added many farm products to the list of protected goods. The final bill sought to reduce federal income partly by permitting some items to enter free and partly by imposing very steep rates on other items to discourage their importation altogether. The provisions for sugar and tinplate illustrate the differing approaches included in the bill.

Most sugar consumed in the United States was imported, and raw sugar produced more tariff revenue than any other import, accounting for nearly a quarter of all tariff receipts in the 1888–89 fiscal year. The McKinley bill put unrefined sugar on the free list. This provision had the additional political advantage that it hurt Louisiana sugar growers, nearly all of whom were Democrats, and therefore put Democrats into the politically awkward position of opposing a major tariff reduction. The bill also provided a federal subsidy of two cents per pound to domestic sugar producers to compensate them for losing the tariff protection that had kept their prices well above those in world markets. By substituting a subsidy for protection, the bill thereby spent part of the budget surplus while not generating federal income on sugar imports. These provisions also ended the advantage enjoyed by Hawaiian sugarcane growers since the mid-1870s, when their product had been exempted from the tariff. This, in turn, contributed indirectly to efforts by Hawaiian growers and entrepreneurs to annex Hawaii to the United States. Conversely, by removing the Hawaiians' advantage, the measure prompted an expansion of Cuban sugar growing and increased Cuban growers' dependence on American markets.

The McKinley bill treated tinplate very differently. At the time, there was no domestic tinplate industry in the United States—all tinplate was imported. The expansion of the canning industry in the 1880s had brought a huge demand for tinplate and generated large tariff revenues on the metal, even though the import rates on it were relatively low. The duty was so low, in fact, that it provided no protection to those interested in producing tinplate domestically. The McKinley bill doubled the tariff, in an effort to encourage the development of a domestic tinplate industry and to reduce imports. Democrats attacked the provision on the grounds that it would substantially increase the cost of canned food. In response, the Republicans added an amendment specifying that tinplate could enter free after 1897 if no domestic tinplate industry developed in the meantime.

In addition to adjusting tariff rates, the McKinley bill, at the urging of Blaine, now secretary of state for the second time, included an offer of reciprocal tariff reduction. Blaine had long advocated increased trade with Latin America, and he urged that the McKinley bill offer to reduce tariff rates on the goods of any nation that reduced its rates on goods from the United States. Harrison gave his backing to the concept.

The House passed the McKinley Tariff in late May and sent it on to the Senate. At the same time, the Republicans were also tackling the problem of the surplus precisely in the way that Cleveland had most feared—by spending it. Republicans had denounced Cleveland for his efforts to limit pensions to Union veterans. They did not falter now that they had the opportunity to demonstrate their generosity to this significant group of voters—who made up 12 to 15 percent of all voters in New York and Indiana. Harrison chose James R. Tanner, head of the New York GAR, for commissioner of pensions. Tanner exclaimed "God help the surplus" and promised to "drive a six-mule team through the Treasury." Such outspokenness cost Tanner his new job within a few months, but, through the Dependent Pension Act, Republicans changed pension eligibility rules to do much of what Tanner had promised.

The new pension law, which passed by near unanimity in both houses, opened pension eligibility to anyone who had served in the army for at least ninety days and was sufficiently disabled for any reason that he could not earn a living by manual labor. Children, parents, and widows of veterans also became eligible for benefits. The number of pensioners grew by 43 percent within four years, and federal pension expenditures nearly doubled, from $80 million during fiscal year 1887–88 to $159 million in fiscal year 1892–93. The pension system had begun as a way to care for those whose service to the Union had rendered them unable to earn their own living. It became, as a result of the workings of party politics, a system of government largess open to the families of the very large number of men who had, however briefly, taken up arms for the Union.

The Republicans also used the surplus to begin construction of a modern navy. The navy had deteriorated badly after the Civil War. Though the initial steps in the direction of a revival of the fleet came under Arthur and Cleveland, the most basic changes came in the Harrison administration, when Benjamin F. Tracy served as secretary of the navy. Congress did not give Tracy all he wanted for naval expansion, but it more than doubled naval appropriations, from $21 million for fiscal year 1888–1889 to nearly $50 million for 1892–93. Included in the construction were the nation's first battleships. In 1889, the U.S. Navy had stood somewhere between 12th and 17th in size among the world's navies; by 1893, it held 7th place and was moving up. Tracy accomplished not just a substantial increase in appropriations for ship construction, but also a shift in the thinking of naval officials and strategists, from emphasizing coastal defenses to envisioning and beginning to build a fleet able to fight in distant seas.

The Republicans did not limit themselves to the problems of the surplus and the tariff. Since 1875, Democrats' numbers in Congress, especially the House, had made futile any Republican effort to carry out their platform pledges to restore full suffrage and honest elections in the South. Many Republicans had taken those pledges seriously, however, and their number included Harrison. Now the House approved the Federal Elections Bill, denounced by Democrats as a "Force Bill." Proposed by Representative Henry Cabot Lodge, a Massachusetts Republican, the bill would have permitted federal judges, upon request of 100 voters in a congressional district, to establish federal supervision to prevent fraud, violence, or disfranchisement in congressional elections. The bill did not single out the South, but everyone understood that the South formed its chief target. The measure passed the House on July 2, 1890, and went on to the Senate where the Republican majority seemed likely to approve.

The Senate, in the meantime, approved two measures named for Senator John Sherman of Ohio: the Sherman Antitrust Act and the Sherman Silver Purchase Act. The Antitrust Act, which Harrison signed on July 2, was the most significant measure passed that year. Although Sherman's name was attached to the act, it actually resulted from the work of the Senate Judiciary Committee, especially George Edmunds of Vermont and George Hoar of Massachusetts, both Republicans and both close associates of the president. Cleveland's tariff message in 1887 had pointed to the dangers of monopoly, and all major parties' platforms in 1888 had condemned the great concentrations of economic power—"trusts" and "monopolies"—that had developed during the 1880s. Cleveland had argued for competition as the solution, but the Sherman Act took a different approach, declaring that "every contract, combination in the form of trust or otherwise, or conspiracy, in restraint of trade or commerce among the several states, or with foreign nations, is hereby declared to be illegal." The Senate approved the Sherman Act by 52–1, and it passed the House with no opposition.

The law made the United States the first industrial nation to attempt to limit business combinations. Harrison did little to implement it, but federal district attorneys did initiate seven antitrust suits during his administration. The most important of the early cases came shortly after the formation, in 1892, of the American Sugar Refining Company, which monopolized nearly all sugar refining in the nation. Most agreed that the Sherman Antitrust Act had been written to prevent such a manufacturing monopoly. However, in *United States* v. *E. C. Knight Co.* (1895), the Supreme Court ruled that the law could not be applied to the actual process of sugar manufacturing, which took place entirely within one state and therefore did not fall under the constitutional power of Congress over *inter*state commerce.

The other measure named for Sherman, the Sherman Silver Purchase Act, was an effort by the Republicans to mollify the western wing of their party. The Bland-Allison Act of 1878 had compromised on the silver issue by requiring the Treasury Department to buy $2–4 million worth of silver each month and coin it into dollars. Because it left gold in a preferential position, it failed to satisfy the advocates of inflation. Because it permitted the coining of silver dollars, it was opposed by those who favored the gold standard. Increased silver coinage found support not just among farmers who wanted inflation but also among representatives—mostly Republicans—of western silver-mining states. In 1890, the Senate passed a measure for unlimited silver coinage, but Reed and McKinley defeated it in the House. In response, silver Republicans threatened to block other party measures, especially the McKinley tariff bill and the Lodge elections bill, until something were done on behalf of silver. The Sherman Silver Purchase Act required the Treasury to buy more silver, 4.5 million ounces per month, roughly equal to the existing production, at market value and to coin it into dollars. It represented a crucial intraparty compromise—most western Republicans considered it the best they could get at the time, and those who opposed silver looked upon it as a necessary compromise for the moment. Harrison signed it into law on July 14, 1890.

Only the tariff and elections bills remained. Harrison wanted them approved as a party package, fulfilling their platform promises. Some Senate Republicans, however, feared that a Democratic filibuster against the elections bill would prevent passage of either measure. Finally a compromise emerged: if Republicans put off the elections bill until the second session, the Democrats would stop delaying the tariff bill. The deal was made, over the strong protests of a few New England Republicans, and Harrison signed the McKinley Tariff on October 1.

The disability pension act, the tariff, the antitrust act, and the silver purchase act were only the most important of a long list of legislation that the Republicans cranked through the first session of the Fifty-first Congress. In all, in ten months, Congress passed a record number of new laws, including admission of Idaho and Wyoming as states (Montana, North Dakota, South Dakota, and Washington had been admitted during the lame-duck session of 1889), organization of territorial government in Oklahoma, creation of the first national forest reserves, and revision of laws to curtail fraud regarding federal lands. In 303 days, the Republicans had virtually enacted their 1888 platform into law. With the exception of the elections bill, the Republicans proved their ability to govern and their willingness to use the power of government. Harrison worked more closely with Republican congressional leaders than any president in anyone's memory. After the fourteen-year partisan deadlock, Republicans hoped—and Democrats feared—that they had broken the political logjam.

CHAPTER THREE

Political Upheaval, 1890–1900

Political scientists and historians who study American politics have discerned between the 1790s and the 1960s five long-term periods of stability in voting behavior, including both voters' choices among parties and turnout, and in many federal policies. Each stable period has lasted about thirty-five years, and each was initiated and ended by a short-term period of change. These long-term periods of stability have been termed "party systems" or "electoral systems." The short-term periods of change have been called "critical elections" or "critical realignments." Though this analytical construct has attracted some criticism, it has proven quite durable as a way to understand large patterns in American political history.

This interpretive framework for American political history designates the years 1860–1896 as the third party system and 1890–1896 as a period of critical realignment. Even those who reject the party systems and critical realignments analysis usually agree that the 1890s were a time of important and far-reaching political change, marking the end of one pattern of politics and the emergence of one different in many ways.

The key element in a realignment is the movement of some voters from one party to another. Since the 1830s, most voters have maintained a standing commitment to one major party or the other. In the late nineteenth century, such party loyalties were at their highest measurable levels. Since the 1890s, party loyalty has been less intense, but a majority of the voters—usually a very large majority—have nonetheless committed themselves to a party. A voter's permanent change from one party to another can be thought of as involving three stages: (1) dissatisfaction with one's own party so strong as to prompt consideration of crossing party lines; such dissatisfaction is often associated with some traumatic event or series of events, e.g., the escalation of the slavery issue in the 1850s or serious economic depression in the 1890s and 1930s; (2) an initial, perhaps tentative, crossing of party lines; and (3) a decision to stay with the new party permanently, based on continuing dissatisfaction with one's previous party and on some confirmation that the new party better fits one's principles and interests.

Not all voters who are dissatisfied with their party proceed through all three stages, and not all who do so move in the same direction. Thus, during a realigning phase, some voters may leave their party only temporarily, some may permanently leave party A to vote for party B and vice versa, some may cease to vote at all, and some who had not previously done so may begin to vote. Realignment does not require that large numbers of voters change parties. It can occur, in fact, if a relatively few voters change parties in an otherwise closely balanced party system.

As a result of voters' choices, old parties may die and new ones may be born, as occurred in the 1820–1830s and in the 1850s, or the balance between the major parties may change significantly, as in the 1930s, when the Democrats went from the minority to the majority, or both parties may change internally without greatly affecting the overall balance between the two. Third parties have sometimes played a significant role in realignments, for some voters find it easier to move to a new party than to change to a party that they had long opposed. In the 1850s, for example, the new Republican party supplanted the Whigs. In 1924, by contrast, the Progressive campaign of that year proved to be a way-station for some urban and working-class voters alienated from both major parties, some of whom eventually moved to the Democrats in the 1930s. The 1890s saw the emergence of one of the most significant third parties in American history, the Populists.

The final element in realignment is change in political leadership, the parties' stands on issues, and federal policies. Changes in voting behavior are relatively easy to identify, but it is more difficult to establish clear causal connections between changes in voting behavior and changes in political leadership and federal policies. Nonetheless, critical election theory, especially as outlined by the political scientist Walter Dean Burnham, posits that changes in political leadership are likely to result during or after a critical realignment because movement by voters between the two major parties changes each party's internal dynamics—by diluting the significance of those constituent groups whose members leave a party and increasing the importance of others whose members join a party. To maintain the loyalty of its new adherents, each party makes room for their representatives in its leadership and incorporates at least some of their concerns into its overall approach to governing, with the majority party able to alter public policy to reflect the concerns of its new supporters. A realigning phase is therefore often followed by changes in some federal policies—e.g., the adoption of an economic policy of distribution (the protective tariff and land grants, discussed in Chapter 1) by the Republicans in 1861–62. Such changes in leadership and policy, in turn, confirm to party switchers that they have the made the right decision, and they therefore stay with their new party and bring into existence a new set of long-term, stable alignments.

The realignment of the 1890s involved five central elements: (1) the emergence of the Populist party in 1890–92 in the West and South; (2) widespread Republican losses in 1889–92 throughout much of the nation; (3) a sweeping Democratic victory in the 1892 election, followed by deep divisions within the Democratic party and a major change in party leadership in 1896; (4) a Republican resurgence centered in the nation's urban-industrial core region, leading to a convincing presidential victory in 1896 and to Republican dominance of national politics until the 1930s; and (5) changes in voting behavior (both party preference and turnout), changes in political structure and process, the emergence of urban reform (presaging progressivism), and the emergence of new policies and issues.

The Emergence of Populism, 1890–1892

Between late 1889 and 1892, the winds of political change blew strongly in the farm communities of the western Midwest and the South and in the mining camps of the Rocky Mountain region, as those regions witnessed the advent of a new political party, the People's party or Populists. The new party grew out of the grievances of some farmers and urban wage earners, and it drew upon the experiences of the grangers, the Greenbackers, the Knights of Labor, the labor parties of the late 1880s, and the Farmers' Alliances. Although there is no direct correlation between voting patterns for the granger parties or Greenbackers and those for the Populists, there is a direct line of development in terms of the ideas and objectives of those organizations.

Since the Civil War, farmers had suffered from declining crop prices. Those prices fell steadily, following the fluctuations of supply and demand both within the United States and elsewhere in the world. Not all farmers accepted the conclusion that prices fell because production had increased more rapidly than the population. Some looked at the hungry and ragged residents of urban slums and asserted that the problem was not overproduction but underconsumption.

Farmers also condemned the monopolistic practices of the grain or cotton buyer. Commodity markets in Chicago or New York determined the prices offered for crops in Kansas. In most agricultural regions, there was only one buyer, who paid prices set by brokers in distant cities. When farmers sold their crops, they accepted the price the buyer offered because most of them needed cash to pay their debts and few of them had the ability to store their crops for later sale at a better price. They knew that a bushel of corn that they had sold for ten cents to a buyer in Kansas brought much more in Chicago or New York, and they blamed grain and cotton brokers for this disparity.

The railroad companies also angered farmers, who relied on them to carry their crops to market and to bring supplies in return. As was true in the 1870s for the grangers, many farmers in the late 1880s saw the railroads as greedy monopolies that conspired to charge as much as possible, knowing that the many small rural shippers had no option but to pay whatever they charged. In some instances, it cost four times as much per pound to ship something a given distance in the West as it cost per pound to ship the same thing over the same distance in the East. While farmers usually acknowledged that it was expensive for railroads to stop every ten miles or so to load grain or cotton, they argued that this factor alone could not justify the large rate differentials.

Critics of railroads addressed more than their rates. Western farmers complained that the railroads, having received vast land grants from the public domain, now refused to pay their fair share of taxes on the land. They protested the railroad companies' involvement in politics and the way their representatives dominated party conventions and state legislatures. Furthermore, railroads commonly distributed free passes to politicians, officeholders, prominent lawyers, newspaper editors, and ministers, a practice the farmers condemned as a form of bribery. The editor of one North Carolina farmers' periodical, in 1888, bemoaned the power of the railroads: "Do they not own the newspapers? Are not all the politicians their dependents? Has not every Judge in the State a free pass in his pocket? Do they not control all the best legal talent in the State?"

Depressed crop prices and railroad practices were only two of the farmers' complaints. They also protested that local banks charged 8, 9, or 10 percent interest—or even more—on loans to farmers in western and southern states, as compared to 6 percent or less charged on farm loans in the Northeast. (Before the Federal Reserve determined interest rates, individual lenders set rates based on the degree of risk involved with each loan, a practice limited only by state usury laws.) Farmers argued that federal monetary policies contributed to deflation and thereby compounded their debts. Some condemned the tariff for protecting manufacturers against competition from foreign imports and thereby creating artificially high prices on manufactured goods that the farmers had to buy, while doing nothing for farmers who had to sell their crops abroad and who remained, therefore, at the mercy of international cotton and grain markets. Farmers complained that the giant corporations that made farm equipment and fertilizer overcharged them. Even local merchants drew farmers' reproach for charging too much. In the South, where all these problems combined with the sharecrop and crop-lien systems, many farmers were so deeply in debt they saw little prospect of ever getting out.[1]

As individuals, farmers could not influence what the railroads charged for hauling their crops to market, nor the price the buyer offered for their crops, nor the cost of fertilizer, nor the amount of interest on their loans. The example of the Grange, however, had demonstrated the importance of collective action when confronting concentrated economic power. The decline of the Grange after the late 1870s left farmers without a strong collective voice. By the mid- or late 1880s, three organizations emerged in its place, all called Farmers' Alliances. The National Farmers' Alliance, centered in the western Midwest, was usually called the Northern Alliance. A second group, usually called the Southern Alliance, originated in Texas and spread eastward across the South, absorbing similar local groups along its way, changing its official name several times in the process, but always limiting its membership to white farmers. The Colored Farmers' Alliance began as an adjunct

---

1 Sharecropping was a form of farm tenancy most widespread in the South, whereby the tenant paid, as rent, a share of the growing crop. The crop lien was a lien placed against a growing crop by a merchant in return for extending credit. Often the landlord and merchant were the same person. Sharecrop leases and crop liens often required the tenant-debtor to turn over the crop at harvest time to the landlord-merchant, who was to market the crop, deduct the landlord's shares and the amount owed the merchant, and then remit the remainder to the tenant farmer. Often there was not enough even to pay what was owed the merchant, much less anything to be returned to the tenant. In such cases, the lease or lien often specified that the lease or lien would continue until the tenant was clear of any debt. In addition, leases and lien often specified that the tenant farmer should grow only cotton, thus increasing the region's dependence on a single crop. To the landlord-merchant, requiring cotton made sense because the tenant farmer might hold back part of any food crop for personal consumption, something not possible with cotton.

to the Southern Alliance, for black farmers. Like the Knights of Labor, the Alliances defined themselves through the concept of the "producing classes" and reasoned that they should receive the full value of their labor. Like the Grange before them and like the Knights of Labor, they looked to cooperatives as a partial solution to farmers' problems. Alliance stores were most common, but the Texas Alliance experimented with cooperative cotton selling, and some midwestern local Alliances built cooperative grain elevators. In cooperative selling, farmers tried to hold their crops back from market in order to negotiate jointly with brokers over prices rather than to accept individually whatever price was offered. The Dakota Alliance also set up cooperative insurance programs for farmers.

Local Alliance meetings featured social and educational activities. The educational program sometimes presented information on new agricultural techniques but sometimes focused on political topics, discussing a wide range of collective concerns and possible remedies. By the late 1880s, a host of weekly newspapers across the South and Midwest presented Alliance views. One Kansas woman described the results of all this discussion and agitation of issues:

People commenced to think who had never thought before, and people talked who had seldom spoken. . . . Everyone was talking and everyone was thinking. Despite the poverty of the country, the books of Henry George, Bellamy, and other economic writers were bought as fast as the dealers could supply them. They were bought to be read greedily; and nourished by the fascination of novelty and the zeal of enthusiasm, thoughts and theories sprouted like weeds after a May shower.

Like the Grange before them, the Alliances defined themselves as nonpartisan and specified that their members should work for Alliance aims from within the major parties. This was especially important in the South, where any white person who challenged the dominant Democratic party ran the risk of being treated as a traitor to both race and section. Many midwestern Alliance leaders, however, continued the granger party tradition and some took part in the Greenback efforts of the 1880s. Not until the winter of 1889–1890, however, did widespread farmer support materialize for independent political action in the Midwest. At this point, corn prices had fallen so low that some farmers found it cheaper to burn their corn than to sell it and buy fuel. A few local Alliances ran their own local tickets in the fall of 1889, and some of their candidates won. All that winter, local Alliance meetings hummed with talk of political action.

In the next spring and summer, Alliance members in Kansas, Nebraska, the Dakotas, Minnesota, and surrounding states broke with the major political parties, charging them with failure to relieve the farmers' woes. They formed new political parties to contest state and local elections. In some places they called themselves the People's party, in others they ran on the Independent or Alliance ticket, but soon they were all called the People's party or Populists (from the Latin word *populus*, meaning people). One of their leaders explained that the political battle they waged was "between the insatiable greed of organized wealth and the rights of the great plain people."

Parades of farm wagons passed down the hot, dusty main streets of scores of country towns to launch the new party. Such parades usually ended with a picnic and rally, where speakers decried the plight of the farmer and proclaimed the sacred cause of the new party. Women took a prominent part in Populist campaigning, especially in Kansas and Nebraska. Newspapers widely quoted one Kansas woman, Mary E. Lease, as telling farmers to "Raise less corn and more hell!" Alliance newspapers throughout the region published new words to familiar songs, such as this one sung to the tune of "Save a Poor Sinner Like Me":

> "I was once a tool of oppression,
> And as green as a sucker could be
> And monopolies banded together
> To beat a poor hayseed like me.
>
> "The railroads and old party bosses
> Together did sweetly agree;
> And they thought there would be little trouble
> In working a hayseed like me. . . .

> "But now I've roused up a little
> And their greed and corruption I see . . .
> And the ticket we vote next November
> Will be made up of hayseeds like me."

The Populists emphasized three elements in their platforms, speeches, and various campaign materials: antimonopolism, government action on behalf of farmers and workers, and increased popular control of government. Their antimonopolism drew upon their own experiences with railroads, grain buyers, and the companies that manufactured farm equipment and supplies. It derived as well from a long American tradition of opposition to concentrated economic power, a tradition whose champions included Thomas Jefferson and Andrew Jackson. The Populists' 1892 platform described the consequences of monopoly power: "The fruits of the toil of millions are boldly stolen to build up colossal fortunes for a few, unprecedented in the history of mankind." The same platform put the blame where any Jacksonian would approve: "From the same prolific womb of governmental injustice we breed the two great classes—tramps and millionaires."

Their solution to the dangers of monopoly proceeded in part from the concept of the producing classes and the cooperative movement. At a local level, they favored formation of producers' and consumers' cooperatives. At a national level, they called for action on behalf of farmers and workers—for federal ownership of the railroads and of the telegraph and telephone systems and for government-run alternatives to private banks. "We believe the time has come," they proclaimed in 1892, "when the railroad companies will either own the people or the people must own the railroads." Their 1892 platform also demanded inflation—through greenbacks, silver, or both—and a graduated income tax to replace the tariff. Though not accepted by all, many Populists, especially in the South, supported a plan developed by the Texas Alliance for the federal government to create storage facilities for farmers' produce and then to make low-interest loans to the farmers with the stored crops as collateral. The Populists had a significant following within what remained of the Knights of Labor, and they hoped to gain broad support among urban and industrial workers—their platform called for the eight-hour day for workers and for prohibition of private armies like that recently used by Carnegie's steel company against its striking workers in Homestead, Pennsylvania.

Finally, they favored structural changes intended to make government more responsive, including expansion of the merit system for government employees, direct election of U.S. senators, a one-term limit for the president, the secret ballot, and the initiative and referendum (which permitted voters to initiate legislation directly through petitions and to attempt to void laws passed by the legislature). Many favored woman suffrage and helped to approve it in statewide votes in Colorado in 1893 and Idaho in 1896.

The Populists thus brought together two major—and sometimes conflicting—strands in American political thinking. One was the distrust of private monopoly that had provoked Andrew Jackson's attack on the Bank of the United States in 1832 and which continued to fuel Democrats' opposition to the tariff and to subsidies. The other was the Republicans' willingness to use the powers of government to accomplish economic objectives. But where the Republicans used the powers of government to stimulate economic growth, and where the Democrats feared that a powerful government would be used only to benefit those already privileged, the Populists wanted to use government to control—even to own—the corporate behemoths that had evolved in their lifetimes. They added a commitment to increasing the direct role of the voter in political decision making, an antiparty attitude derived largely from their distrust of the old parties.

The new party first emerged in 1890, halfway through Harrison's term as president. They contested local and state offices in several states—Kansas, Nebraska, the Dakotas, Minnesota, Colorado, Michigan, and Indiana—scoring their greatest victories in Kansas and Nebraska. In Kansas, U.S. Senator John J. Ingalls had dismissed them at first as "a sort of turnip crusade," but the Kansas Populists elected five members to the House of Representatives, won control of the state legislature, and then elected a Populist to the Senate to replace Ingalls. Populists took two of the three congressional seats in Nebraska, secured majorities in the state legislature, and nearly won the governorship. In South Dakota, they held the balance of power in the legislature and elected another U.S. senator. All across the South, where there were no separate Populist tickets, the Alliance worked to nominate sympathetic Democrats and, after election day, claimed that many of the successful candidates for Congress and for state offices owed their victories to Alliance voters.

Republican Waterloo, 1889–1892

In 1890, Populists achieved most of their gains in regions where the Republicans had usually won lop-sided majorities in election after election. In 1890, Democrats sometimes helped the Populists, either by endorsing the Populists' candidates outright or by running no serious campaign of their own. But the Republicans in 1890 faced many more difficulties than those posed by the angry farmers of Kansas and Nebraska. The presidential campaign of 1888 had papered over some of the party's internal problems, as party leaders and voters focused on the presidency and ignored local concerns. Republicans could not fail to understand the seriousness of their problem, however, when they lost the Iowa governorship in 1889. Few states had been more solidly Republican."Iowa will go Democratic when Hell goes Methodist," proclaimed one Republican campaigner in 1885, although Methodists in 1889 apparently received no upsurge in conversions from the nether regions.

Much of the Republicans' predicament in Iowa stemmed from the close identification of the Iowa state GOP with temperance. Iowa's voters added prohibition to the state constitution in 1882, but it was challenged in court. In 1883, the Republican lieutenant governor proclaimed that "Republicanism" meant "a school house on every hill, and no saloon in the valley," and, in the mid-1880s, the Republican state legislature passed several laws designed to stanch the flow of liquor into the state. These Republican proclivities for temperance alienated some voters, especially German and Danish immigrants and their descendants, many of whom had supported the Republicans but still enjoyed an occasional visit to the saloon in the valley. Another part of the Republicans' difficulties in Iowa came from the growth of agrarian discontent, producing an on-again, off-again coalition between the state Farmers' Alliance and the Democrats.

The Republican vote dropped off not just in Iowa but across the Midwest in 1889 and 1890, and in most places the losses stemmed largely from ethnocultural issues. Republicans had drawn strength from their identification with virtue and morality and had attracted most old-stock Protestant voters outside the South.[2] These Protestants in the North had kindled much of the drive against slavery and had contributed significantly to the postwar defense of the freed people and the extension of citizenship and rights to them during Reconstruction. In the 1880s, the increasingly vigorous temperance movement, spearheaded by the WCTU, appealed strongly to many old-stock Protestants and thereby placed Republican leaders on the horns of a dilemma: if they satisfied the temperance forces, they risked antagonizing Republican voters who did not support prohibition, especially midwestern German Protestants; if they ignored the temperance forces, they risked losing dry voters to the Prohibition party. This problem was especially thorny given the very close balance between the parties in crucial states. In 1884, following three years of Arthur's serving of wine at White House dinners, the Prohibitionists secured enough votes in New York state to hold the balance—and therefore to give the state (and, hence, the presidency) to Cleveland.

The temperance issue had particular significance in Iowa, due to the positions taken by the state Republican party, but it echoed throughout the Midwest as Democrats everywhere scourged Republicans as closet prohibitionists. As J. Sterling Morton of Ne-

---

2 "Old stock" is a census term used to designate people born in the United States of parents born in the United States. As used here, it refers to people whose family had been in the United States for several generations. Old-stock Protestant churches included the Methodists, Presbyterians, Congregationalists, Baptists, and smaller denominations drawing upon the religious heritage of Calvin, Wesley, or the Great Awakening.

braska explained, he campaigned assiduously "to direct the German mind" toward the "peculiar type of mental and moral man"—i.e., Republicans—who advocated prohibition. In 1889, in both Illinois and Wisconsin, Republicans compounded these difficulties by putting through compulsory school attendance laws that required schools to be taught in English, thereby challenging the state's many German-language schools sponsored by Lutheran and Catholic churches. In response, in Milwaukee municipal elections in April 1890, the Republican vote in German Lutheran neighborhoods fell from 53 percent to 25 percent, and similar losses came in German areas in Illinois.

While temperance and school issues contributed to Republican losses in the Midwest, Republican fortunes in the South plummeted for entirely different reasons. There Republicans had continued to win and hold office in some areas based primarily on the votes of African Americans. A few southern congressional districts sent African-American Republicans to Congress throughout the 1880s. In 1888, the Harrison campaign had entertained serious hopes of carrying one or more southern states and had come very close in Virginia. In 1889, encouraged by the Republican control of Congress and Harrison's support for the Lodge elections bill, the Republican party showed more vitality in the South than it had since the end of Reconstruction.

Democrats quickly struck back. The 1889 Democratic campaign in Virginia produced a smashing victory by means so unprincipled that it helped to convince many Republicans of the need for a new Enforcement Act. Other states took different routes to the same end, however, seeking to repress the southern GOP legally. As one Mississippi Democrat put it in 1890, "There must be devised some legal defensible substitute for the abhorrent and evil methods on which white supremacy lies." In the end, southern Democrats accomplished by legislation and constitutional amendment what they had not done with rifle clubs, riots, and ballot-box stuffing—they eliminated the Republican party from southern politics by disfranchising African-American voters.

Some southern states had already begun to experiment with legislation to restrict black voting. Virginia and Georgia experimented with poll taxes in the 1870s. Payment of a poll tax as a requirement for voting posed a potentially difficult barrier in the cash-poor South, where the prevalence of sharecropping and the crop-lien system meant that nearly all access to cash for tenant farmers came at the sufferance of the landlord. South Carolina in 1882 adopted a requirement for eight separate ballots, to be matched to and deposited into eight separately labelled ballot boxes. Voting officials disregarded any ballot placed in the wrong box—a more likely occurrence among black voters than whites, given widespread illiteracy among the poor of both races and the willingness of white officials to provide guidance for white voters. Florida took a similar step in 1889, and Tennessee adopted its secret-ballot law that same year.

Mississippi Democrats took a bolder step in 1890, holding a state constitutional convention to eliminate political participation by African Americans. No Mississippian quite knew how to word such a constitutional provision without mentioning race—which would have violated the Fourteenth and Fifteenth amendments. In the end, they devised a series of barriers to voting, including a two-year residency requirement (intended to disfranchise those who moved most, thought to be young African Americans), payment of a poll tax for the previous two years (which most sharecroppers could not afford), and the passing of a literacy test (which, due to the limited educational opportunities afforded Mississippians, many could not pass). Those who failed the literacy test, however, could still vote if they could understand a section of the state constitution or law after a local official read it to them. Since the local officials were invariably white, in practice this often meant that white illiterates made it through the "understanding" provision but not those who were black. Though legally phrased to apply to all voters, everyone understood that these measures were intended to disfranchise black voters. One critical newspaper complained that the state's "very Constitution" had become "the instrument and shield of fraud."

In contesting the 1890 elections, Democrats everywhere joined local issues (prohibition and English-language laws in the Midwest, the Lodge elections bill in the South) with attacks on the

McKinley Tariff, charging it with producing higher prices. In fact, the tariff would have reduced many consumer prices—it should have reduced sugar prices for consumers by as much as one-third—but those provisions did not take effect until after the election. In the meantime, many eager merchants and manufacturers handed the Democrats a ready-made campaign by increasing prices or cutting wages and blaming it on the new tariff. One canning company, for example, posted a notice of wage reductions and attributed it to the new tariff on tinplate—even though the new rate had not yet taken effect and the nation had a more-than-ample supply of tinplate at previous prices. Eight months before the tariff took effect, some tinware dealers increased prices by 15 to 20 percent. Democrats knew a good thing when they saw it, and they widely publicized such price increases.

Everywhere Republicans found themselves on the defensive, and everywhere they suffered defeat. The Fifty-first Congress (elected in 1888) counted 166 Republicans and 159 Democrats in the House of Representatives. By contrast, in the Fifty-second Congress (elected in 1890), the House had 88 Republicans, 235 Democrats, and 9 Populists. The Democrats' majority was the largest in nearly sixty years. Republicans lost congressional seats all across the country. Facing reelection in a district gerrymandered by Democratic state legislators, McKinley himself went down to defeat. So did other Republican congressional leaders. What happened to the Republicans' congressional candidates also affected their candidates for state and local offices, especially in the Midwest. Given Republican accomplishments in the Fifty-first Congress, many party leaders felt they did not deserve their defeat. Lodge, for example, found the "sting of defeat" especially galling because he felt that "never since the war" had the Republicans presented such a strong record in an election campaign.

Republican disappointment in the results of the 1890 elections bred dissension within the party, and Harrison proved unable to maintain even a semblance of party unity. Some silver-supporting Republicans abandoned Lodge's elections bill when Congress reconvened, apparently in the hope that they might forge an alliance with the South in support of silver. Little of significance came from the second session of the Congress, where everyone seemed to have one eye on the approaching presidential elections of 1892. Each party nominated an experienced presidential candidate in 1892. The Republicans renominated Harrison, despite a lack of enthusiasm among many congressional leaders and a short-lived attempt to stampede the convention to Blaine or McKinley. The Democrats made Grover Cleveland their candidate again. In the South, many Farmers' Alliance activists gave up on the Democratic party and joined the western Populists to form a national People's party. They gave their presidential nomination to James Weaver of Iowa, who had run as a Greenbacker twelve years before.

In many western states, where the Democrats had shrunk to a tiny third party when Populism emerged, they usually gave open or covert support to the Populists as the best means to deny victory to the Republicans. In the South, however, the Democrats viciously attacked the Populists as a threat to white supremacy, whereas southern Republicans sometimes leaned to the Populists as the best means of defeating the Democrats.

Although the Populists did not make a strong showing nationally, they demonstrated strength in three regions: the western Midwest, the Rocky Mountain states, and the South. In these Populist strongholds Weaver carried five states and ran second in nine more. There, too, they elected U.S. congressmen as well as state and local officials. Studies of voting behavior have made clear that Populists were, more than anything else, voting along economic lines rather than those of race, ethnicity, religion, or Civil War loyalties. On the Great Plains, in 1892, Populism appealed most strongly to economically hard-pressed farmers—whether old-stock white Protestants, Irish Catholics, or Scandinavian Lutherans—but it failed to attract more than a few Germans. In Kansas, they made a special appeal to black voters and showed some success. In the Rocky Mountain states, the Populists attracted support not only from farmers but also from labor, especially union members and miners. In Nevada, the leading silver-producing state, former Republicans dominated an independent Silver party that allied with the Populists because of the silver issue. In the South, leading Populists recognized the importance of building a coalition of the poor of both races, and they had some success with their effort, although neither blacks nor whites found the coalition entirely comfortable. All in all, in 1892 Populist gains were striking but limited.

Though the Populist surge attracted a good deal of attention, the Democrats scored the most victories. Cleveland won 46 percent of the popular vote, becoming the only president in American history to serve two nonconsecutive terms. Harrison received 43 percent of the popular vote, and Weaver captured more than 8 percent. The Democrats lost a few congressional seats but kept secure control of the House. For the first time in twelve years, they also won the Senate. The Democrats thus found themselves where the Republicans had stood just four years before: in control of the White House and the Congress and fully able to translate their campaign promises into law.

The Divided Democrats Fail to Govern, 1893–1896

The political realignment that began in 1890 continued through the presidential election of 1896. By an unfortunate coincidence for the Democrats, the nation entered a severe depression in 1893, at almost exactly the same time Grover Cleveland returned to the White House. Cleveland and his party thus confronted not only the silver and tariff issues so central in the 1890 and 1892 elections, but also the challenges posed by the depression. In 1887–1888, late in his first term as president, Cleveland had charted a course on tariff reform only to discover that his party refused to follow it. In that instance, Cleveland had pointed the direction but failed to lead, and he and his party went down to defeat in 1888. Given a second chance by the election of 1892, Cleveland and the Democrats failed even more spectacularly.

Ten days before Cleveland took office, the Reading Railroad declared bankruptcy and a financial panic set in as other companies also plunged into insolvency. The stock market crashed in May and June 1893. One business journal reported, by August, that "never before has there been such a sudden and striking cessation of industrial activity." More than 15,000 businesses failed in

1893, more than ever before in a single year, and more proportionately than since the depression years of 1875–1878.

The depression had begun, in part, when a major English bank collapsed and some British investors called back investments in the United States. This, combined with the decline in tariff revenues caused by the McKinley tariff, produced a decline in federal gold reserves. Major factors underlying the depression also included the end of agricultural expansion and, especially, of railroad construction. Railroad building had driven the industrial economy in the 1880s, but some railroads now found themselves unable to meet their obligations. Several large lines declared bankruptcy, including the Erie, Northern Pacific, Santa Fe, and Union Pacific. By 1894, the ownership of almost one-fifth of the nation's railroad mileage had fallen into bankruptcy. As railroad construction fell by half, demand for steel rails fell by more than a third; thirty-two steel companies eventually closed down. Banks failed too—nearly 500 in 1893 alone, and another 500 by the end of 1897, equivalent to 1 bank out of every 10. At the time, no agency kept careful records on unemployment, but economic historians have since estimated that nearly 3 million workers were unemployed in 1893 and 4.6 million in 1894—12 and 18 percent of the civilian labor force respectively. Those out of work may have included one-third or more of the wage earners in manufacturing.

Few people at the time understood why the economy collapsed so suddenly and so completely. Many Democrats blamed the McKinley Tariff. Gold standard advocates in both parties blamed the Sherman Silver Purchase Act for the gold drain and for discouraging foreign investment. Populists and inflationists blamed the Silver Purchase Act, too, but faulted it for not going far enough to save debt-ridden farmers. Conservatives blamed Populists and radicals for discouraging investment. Samuel Gompers, president of the AFL, blamed the greed of "the capitalist class." The APA blamed Catholics. Henry Adams and some of his friends muttered about a "dark, mysterious" conspiracy.

In the midst of the financial crisis, Cleveland's physicians found cancer in his mouth. Fearing that news of his condition might contribute to further financial panic, the president kept his condition secret. Criticized for taking a "vacation" while the nation's economy was in turmoil, Cleveland actually had left the executive mansion to undergo surgery for the removal of part of his jaw and then had taken some time to recuperate and to learn how to handle a prosthesis.

Before his surgery, Cleveland had become convinced that the Sherman Silver Purchase Act had contributed significantly to the economic collapse. In 1885, during his first term, he had urged Congress to repeal the Bland-Allison Act of 1878, on the grounds that the United States could not, by itself, maintain both gold and silver as money. When Cleveland left the presidency in 1889, the government's gold reserves stood at $197 million. When he resumed office in 1893, the gold reserves had fallen to $103.5 million, dangerously close to the $100 million mark that Congress had earlier fixed as the minimum level necessary to maintain the gold standard. The decline had come partly because of reduced tariff revenues and the increased expenditures approved by the Republicans in 1889–1890, and partly due to economic fears that had led many investors to convert their holdings to gold. The Silver Purchase Act had contributed, too, because it required the monthly purchase of silver by the government. Bankers and manufacturers—and many eastern Democrats—now urged Cleveland to end silver coinage and to restore the gold reserves to their earlier levels. Many Democrats from the South and West, however, had disliked the Silver Purchase Act only because it did not enact unlimited silver coinage, and now they opposed its repeal.

Five weeks after his secret surgery, Cleveland returned to Washington and asked Congress to repeal the Sherman Silver Purchase Act. In the House, most Republicans voted for the act's repeal and the few Populists in that body voted against it. The outcome, therefore, hinged on the Democrats, and Cleveland did what he could, including the use of patronage, to keep members of his party in line for repeal. Nonetheless, more than one-third of the House Democrats defied the president and voted against the repeal. In the Senate, the Republicans supported Cleveland by a 2–1 margin, but the Democrats divided almost evenly. Given the economic situation in 1893, repeal may have been necessary to prevent further economic disaster. Cleveland managed to secure it, but at a significant political cost, dividing his party almost down the middle, pitting most northeastern Democrats against most of those from the West and South. In the fall of 1893, a few states held elections. The Democrats lost not only the gains they had made since 1889 but even some positions that had long been theirs.

Cleveland and the Democrats in Congress also had to contend with the tariff issue, which they had played so effectively for votes in 1890 and 1892. Their 1892 platform had declared that: "the Federal Government has no constitutional power to impose and collect tariff duties, except for the purpose of revenue only, and we demand that the collection of such taxes shall be limited to the necessities of the Government when honestly and economically administered." Despite such Jacksonian pronouncements in favor of a tariff for revenue only, many congressional Democrats took a more moderate stand on the issue. After condemning the McKinley Tariff so vigorously, the Democrats now had to prove they could provide something better.

Late in 1893, the House Ways and Means Committee, under Chairman William L. Wilson, produced a bill that reduced the McKinley duties substantially, putting many raw materials on the free list and cutting rates on most manufactured goods. The bill also introduced an income tax to recover some of the federal revenue to be lost by the reduced tariff. Republicans resorted to the disappearing quorum as a tongue-in-cheek delaying tactic, but the House Democratic leadership—true to the position they had insisted on in 1890—refused to count them and instead relied on their own members to muster a quorum. In February, the House passed the Wilson tariff bill by a vote of 204 to 140, with no Republicans in favor and 17 Democrats against.

The Senate posed a more difficult problem. There Democrats held a thin majority, but the real balance of power rested with a dozen or so Democrats who wanted to protect their state's industries. Led by Arthur P. Gorman of Maryland, Senate Democrats agreed to whatever was required to hold the protectionist members of their party in line. Louisiana Democrats, for example, insisted on moving raw sugar from the free list to a rate of 40 percent. And sugar was not the only commodity for which the Senate Democrats set a higher tariff rate than that of the McKinley Act. The Senate's final vote stood at 37–34, with all Republicans voting no, all Democrats but one voting yes, and the four Populists split 2–2. All in all, the Senate adopted more than six hundred amendments and so altered the Wilson bill that Cleveland scorned the outcome as "party perfidy and party dishonor." House Democrats tried to roll back some of the Senate changes in the conference committee, but Senate conferees were adamant, and the House finally surrendered. Cleveland, however, refused to sign the Wilson-Gorman Tariff, and it became law without his signature. The new tariff provided a disappointing conclusion to Cleveland's bold call for tariff reform from six years before, as well as a vivid illustration of his party's inability to deliver on its platform promises, even when it had the power to do so.

The tariff battle was, as well, yet another instance in which Cleveland failed to lead his party. Cleveland had provided leadership in repealing the Sherman Silver Purchase Act, especially by using patronage to move some members of his own party. When it came to the tariff battle, however, he carped from the sidelines. He did little or nothing to persuade protectionist Democrats in the Senate to accept lower rates, nor did he attack the corporate beneficiaries of protection (as he had done in 1887) as a way of focusing public opinion. Instead, he waited until the Senate had finished with the bill, then lambasted the Democratic protectionists whose support he still needed. Of course, leadership can sometimes involve *not* leading one's troops in a direction they refuse to go. Once Cleveland realized there was no possibility of getting downward tariff revision, he might have worked with House Democrats to delay the issue until after the election. But he neither wooed the protectionist Democrats nor tried to mobilize public opinion nor opted for delay. The result was disaster for his party.

In late April, while Senate Democrats were busily rewriting the Wilson bill, Washington buzzed over the impending arrival of a protest march by the unemployed. The "petition in boots" had begun in late January 1894, when Jacob S. Coxey, an Ohio Populist, proposed that the government hire the unemployed to build roads and other public works, and that it pay them in new greenbacks, thereby stimulating inflation. He called upon the unemployed to join him in marching to Washington to petition Congress for this program. The response shocked some and inspired others. All across the country—but especially in the West—hundreds of men and a few women set out to join "Coxey's Army." Given the vast distances they need to cover, some western groups hijacked trains and, pulling boxcars loaded with unemployed men, headed east, though none made it very far before authorities stopped them and arrested the leaders. Several thousand people participated in the march of Coxey's Army in some way, but most never reached Washington or else reached Washington too late to participate in the actual demonstration.

When Coxey and his group of several hundred arrived in Washington, they learned that he would not be permitted to speak at the Capitol. When he tried to do so anyway, on May 1, police arrested him and two others for carrying political banners and trespassing on the Capitol grounds. Mounted police then used their clubs to disperse the crowd, and the march was over. Nonetheless, Coxey's Army marked the first time that so many protesters had ever gone to Washington, and the first time that so many had called upon the federal government to provide jobs for the unemployed. Reactions were mixed. Conservatives criticized both Coxey's proposals and his actions, one Chicago newspaper claiming that "The country is sick just to the extent that its people try to lean on the government instead of standing upright on their own two feet." Some conservative Democrats compared the Coxeyites, with their demands for governmental assistance, to the beneficiaries of the protective tariff, concluding that both wanted "to be supported . . . at public expense." Only a few prominent public figures, most of them Populists, stepped forward in defense of Coxey and his followers.

Soon after the dispersal of Coxey's Army, Cleveland faced difficult choices when the new American Railway Union (ARU) announced a boycott of Pullman cars. Formed in 1893, under the leadership of Eugene V. Debs, a former officer of the locomotive firemen's union, the ARU recruited all railroad workers and hoped to supersede the separate unions of engineers, firemen, switchmen, and conductors. Within a year, the ARU claimed 150,000 members, making it the largest single union in the nation. Meanwhile, the General Managers Association (GMA), made up of executives of the twenty-four railways that entered Chicago, watched the ARU grow and waited for an opportunity to challenge it.

In 1894, striking workers at the Pullman Company, a manufacturer of luxury railway cars, asked the ARU to boycott Pullman cars—to disconnect them from trains, run them onto sidings, and proceed without them. Endorsing the boycott put the ARU on a collision course with the GMA, which insisted that only managers had authority to determine which cars would make up a train. GMA members agreed to fire any worker who observed the boycott. But as soon as any ARU member was fired for boycotting a Pullman car, other ARU members in that area immediately struck. By late June, strikers had closed down rail traffic in and out of Chicago and blocked rail traffic in states from California to New York. Attorney General Richard Olney, a former railroad lawyer, obtained a court injunction against the strikers on July 2 by arguing that the strike prevented delivery of the U.S. mail and interfered with interstate commerce in violation of the Sherman Antitrust Act. At Olney's urging, Cleveland approved the use of thousands of U.S. marshals and federal troops to protect trains operated by strikebreakers. Mobs in several states lashed out at railroad property, especially in Illinois, where they burned trains and buildings for three days. ARU leaders condemned the violence, but a dozen people died before it ended. Union leaders, including Debs, served short jail terms for refusing to obey the court injunction to end the strike. The ARU collapsed.

Cleveland's actions in the Pullman strike divided his hapless party even further. Marcus A. Hanna, a close political adviser of McKinley, denounced Pullman as "a God damn fool" for refusing to "meet his men half-way," and Cleveland had previously pronounced himself in favor of the peaceful arbitration of labor disputes. In 1894, however, he did nothing to encourage a peaceful resolution. Instead, he seems to have relied solely on the advice of his attorney-general, Richard Olney, and Olney's instinct was to use force. When Cleveland sent federal troops to Illinois, he did so over the strong opposition of the state's Democratic governor, John Peter Altgeld. Debs, the ARU leader, had campaigned vigorously for Cleveland in 1888 and 1892, but Olney sent him to jail anyway. Though Cleveland consistently took positions that conservatives applauded as "principled" and "courageous," he not only failed to unite the increasingly divided Democrats but actually drove them further apart.

At the same time, midway through 1894, William H. Harvey published *Coin's Financial School*, a fictional account of a young silver defender whose logic confounded the most prominent financial and commercial figures of the day. The book's surging sales further boosted the booming silver cause.

The 1894 elections demonstrated the voters' response to the Democrats' failures—they lost everywhere except in the Deep South. Republicans scored the biggest congressional gains ever, adding 117 seats while the Democrats lost 113. Republicans now held nearly all the congressional seats in the Midwest and New England. Democrats lost congressional seats not just in New England and the Midwest, but also in the border states and even in four former Confederate states. As was true for the Republicans in 1890, the Democratic debacle in 1894 also unseated state and local officials. Populists lost too. They had expected to reap major gains from voters' dissatisfaction with the old parties, but they lost important elections in Kansas and Colorado, where Populist governors had taken controversial actions that contributed to their party's defeat, and Populists scored only modest gains elsewhere. They did register gains among some urban working-class voters, among miners and railroad workers, and in the South. Voters seem to have spurned the Democrats out of some combination of concern over the continuing depression and disgust over the party's demonstrated inability to govern. They seem to have rejected the Populists as unproven radicals who might discourage the investment of capital needed to bring recovery. And they seem to have turned to the Republicans as the party with a proven commitment to using the federal government to bring economic growth. Republican leaders now looked forward enthusiastically to the presidential election in 1896.

Although the repeal of the Silver Purchase Act badly damaged the Democratic party, it failed to stanch the flow of gold out of the Treasury. In the face of economic uncertainty, many investors continued to exchange greenbacks, silver certificates, or silver dollars for gold, and the nation's gold reserve became seriously endangered. Under the combined impact of the McKinley tariff and the depression (both of which reduced federal revenues) and the increased federal expenditures voted by the Fifty-first Congress, the federal surplus had disappeared, to be replaced with a federal deficit of $61 million in 1894. More and more demands were placed on the gold reserves, but the Treasury had no way to replenish them. The gold reserves continued to fall until Cleveland began to fear that the Treasury might be unable to make gold payments. He therefore authorized a series of bond issues—a way for the federal government to borrow funds to restore the gold reserves. The first two bond issues, in 1894, staved off the immediate crisis. When a third issue became necessary, early in 1895, Cleveland met personally with J. P. Morgan, the nation's most powerful banker. The conference was tense. Morgan later related that he had held an unlighted cigar in his hand at the onset and discovered, at the end of the conference, that he had unconsciously ground it to powder. A fourth bond issue came in early 1896. The gold reserves were restored, rising above $100 million by the end of February 1896. Though he succeeded, Cleveland once again came under heavy criticism, this time for going to Morgan—symbol of Wall Street and the trusts—to save the nation's credit.

Republican Resurgence and Democratic Downfall: The Battle of the Standards, 1896

The approach of the 1896 presidential election found the Democrats divided over silver and a number of other issues, and many of them dispirited by the repeated failures of their party to establish a record of accomplishment. Having completed two terms, Cleveland made no effort to secure renomination. Given the deep division within his party, he probably could not have been nominated had he wanted to be, nor could he have controlled the convention or determined the nominee. Republicans, by contrast, were jubilant over their successes in 1894 and hopeful that the tariff and currency issues might permit them to mute the difficult ethnocultural issues that had proven their downfall in 1889 and 1890. The Republicans scheduled their convention for mid-June, and the Democrats planned to meet in early July. Populists set their convention for late July, in the expectation that both of the old parties would reject silver and open the door for the Populists to unite the forces of reform by recruiting to their ranks the silverites of both major parties. In addition, in early 1896, three leading national organizations favoring silver coinage joined to call for a Silver party convention following the Republican and Democratic nominating conventions.

By the time the Republicans met, William McKinley had already emerged as the leading candidate. A Union veteran who had risen to the rank of major, he studied law after the war and practiced law in Ohio until winning election to the House of Representatives in 1876. In the House, he emerged as one of the Republican leaders and chaired the Ways and Means Committee in the Fifty-first Congress. Though he lost his congressional seat in 1890, he quickly came back to capture the Ohio governorship in 1891, winning reelection by a large margin in 1893.

McKinley and his campaign manager, Hanna, put together a strong campaign for the presidential nomination, based in the Midwest but with important strength nearly everywhere. Hanna, a retired Ohio industrialist, took good care of organizational details, but the direction of the campaign always rested with McKinley. He liked to portray his campaign as a struggle by the people against party bosses and also delighted in presenting himself as his party's leading tariff expert. He blamed the Wilson-Gorman tariff for the depressed economic conditions of the Cleveland years and wanted to make the tariff his central issue. He straddled the money question until a few days before the convention when he and his advisers agreed to write into the platform a commitment to "the existing gold standard" and, at the same time, acknowledging the prospect for bimetallism through international agreement. Billing himself as the "Advance Agent of Prosperity," he and Hanna had honed their preconvention organization so carefully that McKinley won the party's nomination on the first ballot, by a 3–1 margin over four rivals. When the convention adopted its pro-gold stance, however, a small number of western Republicans, led by Senator

Henry Teller of Colorado, walked out of the convention and out of the party.

The Democratic convention opened a few weeks later. There, advocates of silver coinage outnumbered the defenders of Cleveland's policies, but the silverites were not united behind any one candidate. The platform committee divided sharply on silver coinage, but the majority was in favor. The minority, opposing silver, insisted on a decision by all the delegates, so the committee scheduled a debate on the issue before the full convention. For closing speaker, the committee majority chose William Jennings Bryan of Nebraska.

Born in Illinois, Bryan had practiced law in Nebraska before winning election to the House of Representatives in 1890. By early 1891, he had voiced a regional concern over currency issues: "We simply say to the East," he told a Kansas City crowd, "take your hands out of our pockets and keep them out." Reelected to the House in 1892, he emerged as the most eloquent defender of silver during the debate over the repeal of the Sherman Silver Purchase Act. In 1893, he played a major role—perhaps the key role—in persuading the few Democrats in the Nebraska legislature to help elect a Populist to the U.S. Senate. In 1894, he convinced Nebraska Democrats to endorse the Populists' candidates for most state offices, and this coalition elected a Populist as governor. Bryan hoped that a similar fusion might elect him to the Senate in 1895, but those hopes foundered when Republicans swept the state legislature. He then took a position with the Omaha *World-Herald* as an editorialist and reporter, and he traveled the nation speaking on the silver issue.

The Democratic convention took up the matter of deciding the platform before it turned to nominating candidates. The committee majority designated two of its members to speak in support of silver, Benjamin Tillman of South Carolina and Bryan. Tillman delivered a tiresome, hour-long harangue, then yielded to three speakers who defended Cleveland's gold policies. When the last of the progold speakers had finished, Bryan sprang from his seat, bounded to the platform, raised his right arm, and bade the crowd be quiet. Anticipation flooded the hall as silver delegates waited for Bryan to put their emotions into words. He did not fail them.

Bryan delivered a masterful piece of oratory. Evoking the rhetoric of the Knights of Labor and Farmers' Alliances, he defined the issue as a conflict between "the producing masses" and "the idle holders of idle capital." He then presented a metaphor that his party was to call upon throughout the next century when he argued that the first priority of government economic policy should be "to make the masses prosperous," rather than to benefit the well-to-do in the hopes that "their prosperity will leak through on those below." His closing rang out both defiant and Biblical: "Having behind us the producing masses of this nation and the world, supported by the commercial interests, the laboring interests, and the toilers everywhere, we will answer their demand for a gold standard by saying to them: You shall not press down upon the brow of labor this crown of thorns." Raking his fingers down his temples, Bryan continued, "You shall not crucify mankind upon a cross of gold." As his final words rolled over the crowd he stretched his arms straight out from his sides as if on a cross himself, stood silent for a moment, then let his arms fall to his sides and took a step back. His speech stunned the convention and provoked a half-hour demonstration in support of silver, and of Bryan. Only thirty-six years old and not a declared candidate for the nomination before his speech, Bryan nonetheless took it on the fifth ballot. The winning platform endorsed not only unlimited silver coinage but also tariff reduction and the income tax.

The Populists and the Silver party (usually called the Silver Republicans) held their nominating conventions amidst a general feeling that the Democrats had stolen their thunder. The Populists had expected to reap a bountiful harvest of recruits after both old parties rejected silver. Now they faced a distressing dilemma: to unite the silver forces behind the Democrats and lose their own distinctiveness; or to maintain their separate identity and guarantee a McKinley victory. Given Bryan's commitment to silver, the income tax, and a broad range of reforms that they also favored, and given the close working relationship he had developed with Populists, the Populists gave him their nomination too, and the Silver Republicans followed suit. The Populists, however, nominated Thomas Watson of Georgia for the vice-presidency, hoping that Arthur Sewall, the Democratic candidate, would withdraw and permit the construction of a genuine fusion ticket. Watson yielded to no one in his commitment to Populism and in his dislike for the Democrats who had engaged in fraud on a massive scale to defeat him and his party in Georgia. When Sewall did not withdraw, Watson remained in the race. Bryan thus campaigned with three parties' nominations and two vice-presidential candidates.

In early September, a group of Democrats met in Indianapolis and nominated two Civil War generals, one from each side, to run as candidates of the National Democratic party on a platform that praised Cleveland and the gold standard. Although most of the funding for this splinter party came from the East, their campaign centered in the Midwest and border states. Usually called the Gold Democrats, they had no thought of winning a single state but hoped instead to persuade Democratic voters of the dangers of silver coinage and to draw votes from Bryan. By late October, the Gold Democrats' candidate for president told a gathering in Missouri that he would find no fault with them if they voted for McKinley.

Bryan and McKinley both waged all-out campaigns, but each used sharply contrasting tactics. Many business leaders feared that Bryan and silver coinage would bring complete financial collapse, and they opposed his other proposals such as the income tax and lower tariff rates. Hanna played on such fears to secure donations from business people and amassed a campaign fund of nearly $4 million—more than had ever been raised before, and more than ten times as much as the Democrats raised. The Republican party used these funds to flood the country with speakers, pamphlets, and—for the first time—campaign buttons with a pin attached to the back. McKinley materials and gewgaws spilled forth in such a thundering river that Theodore Roosevelt snorted that Hanna "advertised McKinley as if he were a patent medicine." McKinley himself stayed home in Canton, Ohio, ostensibly to be near his invalid wife. The Republicans chartered trains and brought thousands of their supporters to hear McKinley speak from his front porch. The Republicans wrote off the South and much of the West, assumed that the East was theirs with minimal effort, and identified the Midwest as the crucial battle ground.

Where the McKinley campaign ticked away like precision clockwork, the efforts for Bryan sometimes seemed distinctly amateurish. In the end, Bryan's most important campaign asset proved to be the instrument that had won him the nomination—his voice. Usually accompanied by his wife Mary, he traveled 18,000 miles by train, visited 26 states and more than 250 cities, and spoke to as many as 5 million people between his nomination and election day. News that his train was coming through town invariably brought a crowd to the station, even in the middle of the night. He loved to speak, and he did so virtually every time his train stopped. Everywhere he drove home his central message: the most important issue was silver, and once the silver issue was properly settled other reforms would follow. He found excited and enthusiastic support nearly everywhere his train took him.

Watson, however, became a problem for the Bryan campaign. After Bryan repeatedly announced his confidence in Sewall, Watson suggested that fusion meant "that we play Jonah while they play whale." In most states, the Bryan-Sewall ticket went on the ballot, and Populists received only modest recognition. When the Georgia Populist committee withdrew Watson's name from the ballot in his own state, the stubborn Populist advised a crowd, "There are two tickets you can vote—for Bryan and Sewall, or for McKinley and Hobart; or if you can't stand either you can stay away from the election next Tuesday and not vote at all."

But, unlike Watson, most Populists, especially in the West, put on Bryan buttons and toiled for his cause. Bryan also won important support from leaders of organized labor, especially officers of the Knights of Labor, the United Mine Workers, and the Chicago Building Trades Council. Eugene V. Debs, leader of the Pullman strike of 1894, also gave Bryan his blessing. Bryan could cite a strong and impressive record of opposition to the APA. Although personally a teetotaler, his record against prohibition should have lost him no support among those who liked their beer. Therefore, *if* he could hold the ethnic core of the midwestern Democratic party, *if* he could attract economically distressed farmers and workers, *if* southern Democrats and Populists could set aside local differences during the campaign, *if* the western mining states voted as anticipated, Bryan would triumph. Early in October, a survey by the New York *Herald* indicated that Bryan led in states with 237 electoral votes, a clear majority.

Early Republican campaign polls revealed that McKinley might have difficulty carrying key midwestern states, even his own Ohio. Much of the paper blizzard originating from his Chicago campaign headquarters focused on this crucial territory, as did a last minute blitz of speakers. Hanna sprang his most audacious campaign tactic in the last week of October: calling for a day to display the flag as a symbol of support for McKinley. Bryan responded by asking his supporters to fly the flag too, but as a symbol of patriotism not party. Bryan's rejoinder came late—the McKinley campaign moved into its final days tightly wrapped in the American flag.

During the closing month of the campaign, Bryan devoted much of his time to the Midwest, especially Illinois, Indiana, Michigan, and Ohio, but he proved unable to hold the ethnic core of his party there. In 1894, Bryan had engineered a Democratic-Populist fusion campaign in Nebraska against a Republican opponent well known for his anti-Catholicism—a circumstance that persuaded most conservative Catholic Democrats to vote for the Populist candidate for governor. He had no such advantage against McKinley in 1896. Even before the Republican convention the APA had marked McKinley as the most unacceptable Republican seeking the nomination, and McKinley had condemned the secret order. By election day, McKinley benefited both from support among some Catholics (attracted by his treatment of economic issues or by his condemnation of the APA or both) and from the APA's resigned attitude that the Republican ticket was still preferable to the Democratic. McKinley could also point to support from at least a few labor leaders. Both the gold standard and McKinley's refusal to associate himself with prohibition helped his cause among German voters—one survey indicated that McKinley had the support of 503 of the nation's 581 German-language newspapers. His approach was so broad that it attracted both a Catholic archbishop and the APA, prohibitionists and saloonkeepers, unionists and adamantly antiunion employers.

Election day saw four of every five eligible voters troop to the polls. In closely contested midwestern states—Iowa, Illinois, Indiana, Ohio, Michigan—turnouts of eligible voters reached 95 percent and more. Bryan received 6.5 million votes, more than any previous presidential candidate, but McKinley got even more, 7.1 million. McKinley took 51 percent of the popular vote (making him the first Republican since Grant to carry a popular majority) and carried 23 states with 271 electoral votes. Bryan received just under 47 percent of the popular vote, and won 22 states and 176 electoral votes. In both the popular vote and the electoral vote, McKinley scored the largest margin of victory since 1872. Bryan took the South and nearly all of the West. McKinley's victory came in the northeastern and midwestern manufacturing belt, the region that included most of the urban population and most of the heavy industry. Of the twenty largest cities in the nation, Bryan won a majority only in New Orleans.

The campaign of 1896 had focused on economic issues, and the depression sharpened the significance of economic issues for many voters. Bryan's silver crusade appealed most to debt-ridden farmers and western miners, although he held the loyalty of many ethnic Democrats, especially those of Irish descent. McKinley forged a broader appeal with his emphasis on the protective tariff and the gold standard as keys to economic recovery. One Kansas Republican later claimed that "McKinley won because the Republicans had persuaded the middle class, almost to a man, that a threat to the gold standard was a threat to their prosperity." For many urban residents—workers and the middle class alike—silver seemed only to promise inflation and higher prices. For voters who worked in manufacturing, the protective tariff meant jobs in American factories. Some companies even pressured their employees to vote Republican by announcing that they would shut down if Bryan won, and some loan companies similarly threatened to foreclose loans.

McKinley also won, at least in part, because he put a damper on moral reforms such as prohibition. Playing down ethnic issues and condemning the anti-Catholic APA made it easier for McKinley to win support among Catholics and immigrants—especially

Germans—who liked his stand on the gold standard or the tariff. He also carried the border states, which had usually voted Democratic since the Civil War, aided partly by the Gold Democrats who drew enough votes from conservative Democrats to give Kentucky to McKinley rather than Bryan.

So the battle of the standards came to its end. The great silver crusade was over, though its most enthusiastic supporters long refused to accept defeat. Bryan quickly produced a book about the campaign, which he optimistically entitled *The First Battle*. Republicans, however, had the most reason for optimism. They had not only won a majority of the popular vote for the first time since Grant, twenty-four years before, they had also carried sizable majorities in both houses of Congress. Unlike Bryan, McKinley had no interest in writing a book—he had to pick a cabinet and organize a presidential administration. Neither man, however, had any inkling of the extent to which their campaign marked the end of one political era and the beginning of another.

An End and Many Beginnings

McKinley's victory in 1896 marked not just the beginning of a new Republican administration, but also the beginning of a new party system, a circumstance wholly outside the understanding of the participants at the time. As president, McKinley built upon and extended the pattern Harrison had developed for working closely with Republican leaders in Congress. In 1897, a new protective tariff, the Dingley Tariff, fulfilled Republican campaign promises. It reduced the list of imports that could enter the nation duty-free and drove the rates on certain items higher than they had been under the McKinley Tariff of 1890. In one key House vote, at least 97 percent of the Republicans voted together, as did at least 97 percent of the Democrats—a much higher rate of party cohesion than had usually been the case in tariff votes. The Republicans also tried to prevent a repetition of anything like the Pullman strike through the Erdman Act of 1898, which, for the first time, recognized the legitimacy of railroad unions and provided a federal mechanism to mediate railway labor disputes. The budget surplus disappeared as an issue, primarily as a result of significantly larger federal expenditures. In 1900, the Gold Standard Act wrote the Republicans' commitment to that monetary policy into law, and the congressional vote on the measure broke almost exactly along party lines, unlike the voting on the Bland-Allison or Sherman Silver Purchase acts.

Although issues of domestic economic policy had dominated the campaign of 1896, foreign affairs commanded the most attention during much of McKinley's presidency. He presided over a quick and successful war with Spain in 1898 and over the acquisition of an insular empire that stretched halfway around the world, from Puerto Rico through Hawaii, Samoa, and Guam to the Philippines. Though the Harrison administration laid important groundwork, McKinley's presidency initiated a new era in American foreign relations, in which the nation accepted globe-girdling commitments that necessitated a much more active role in world affairs.

The election of 1900 confirmed the results of 1896. Bryan easily won the Democrats' nomination for a second time, and the Democratic platform strongly condemned the McKinley administration for its "imperialism." Bryan hoped to make imperialism the major issue in the election, but found that many conservative anti-imperialists were unwilling to support him for president because he continued to insist on silver coinage and to attack the trusts and big business. The Republicans renominated McKinley and for vice-president chose Theodore Roosevelt, who had emerged from the war with Spain as the "hero of San Juan Hill." Roosevelt, cavalry hat on his head, carried the brunt of the GOP campaign, including a flag-waving defense of territorial acquisition. Where Bryan repeatedly attacked imperialism, McKinley campaigners took pride in "expansion" (they never used the term "imperialism") and questioned the patriotism of anyone who proposed to pull down the flag where it had once been raised.

McKinley easily won a second term with almost 52 percent of the popular vote to less than 46 percent for Bryan. The electoral vote stood nearly 292–155 in McKinley's favor. McKinley not only carried the states of the Manufacturing Belt that had given him his victory in 1896, but also recovered lost Republican territory in most of the western states where Populism had once flourished—including Bryan's home state, Nebraska. Republicans also won secure majorities in both houses of Congress. In 1896, Bryan and McKinley had fought their first contest in the midst of a depression, with Grover Cleveland in the White House disapproving of both candidates. In 1900, by contrast, McKinley could point not just to a short and highly successful war and to legislation that had fulfilled his party's major campaign promises on the tariff and the gold standard, but to the return of prosperity as well.

Bryan's defeat in 1896 spelled the end of the Populist party as a significant political organization. It lingered on in a few places but split at the national level into two factions in 1900, one endorsing Bryan and the other running a separate candidate, who did poorly. Some Populists moved into the Democratic party, and some returned to the Republicans. A few joined the Socialist party and a few simply ignored politics altogether. The collapse of the Populists meant that no sizable party now spoke for government ownership of railroads and telephone and telegraph systems, for a government-operated alternative to privately owned savings and lending institutions—for a radical approach to the relation between the federal government and big business.[1]

The realignment of the mid-1890s brought significant changes to Congress. Democrats found it more difficult to win elections in some previously competitive districts in the Northeast and Midwest. After the southern states disfranchised black and some poor white voters, it became virtually impossible for Republicans to win elections there. As a consequence, the congressional Democrats became somewhat more homogeneous, with the majority coming from relatively rural areas in the southern and border states. Some prominent western Republicans left their party and never returned, either losing their seats or becoming a part of the Bryan coalition—including Senators Henry Teller of Colorado, Richard Pettigrew of South Dakota, and Fred Dubois of Idaho.

---

1 The Socialist Party of America, formed in 1901, never reached the strength the Populists demonstrated in 1892, and never succeeded in winning governorships and senatorships, although it did win seats both in a few state legislatures and in the House of Representatives.

Newly elected Republicans in the West more closely reflected the priorities of the dominant northeastern and midwestern wing of the party. The realignment, thus, produced more unified parties in Congress.

The McKinley administration ushered in a generation of Republican dominance of national politics. From the mid-1870s to the mid-1890s, neither Democrats nor Republicans could muster a working majority. The parties throughout that period remained stalemated, with neither able to turn its proposals into public policy. After 1896, no one doubted that the Republicans were the national majority. The economic problems of farmers, the depression, and the political campaigns of the 1890s had caused some voters to reevaluate their partisan commitments and to change parties. The urban-industrial core region of the nation—the Northeast and much of the Midwest—became solidly Republican. Republicans formed the majority in the House of Representatives for 28 of the 36 years after 1894, and in the Senate for 30 of those 36 years. Republicans won seven of the nine presidential elections from 1896 to 1932. Similar patterns of Republican dominance appeared in state and local government, especially in the Manufacturing Belt. Only the Deep South and parts of a few northern cities remained Democratic strongholds. In the West, however, enough Populists and Silver Republicans became Bryan Democrats to make some of those states more competitive than they had been before 1890.

In some ways, the realignment of the 1890s produced less dramatic changes than those of the 1850s and 1930s. In the 1850s, realignment yielded a new political party. The realignment of the 1930s saw both a clear shift in majority status and the emergence of organized labor as a significant new element in politics. By contrast, the realignment of the 1890s did not produce massive changes in voter loyalties. Some western Republicans became Democrats, a larger number of midwestern and northeastern Democrats became Republicans, and most southern Republicans were disfranchised.

In some ways, the Democratic party changed very little. Most northern Democrats continued to oppose nativism and moral reform, and southern Democrats continued their commitment to states' rights as they solidified their white supremacist regimes by disfranchising and segregating African Americans. In other ways, the changes of the 1890s were far reaching, most notably in the party's leadership and its position on economic issues. Bryan dominated the Democratic party from 1896 until 1912—sixteen years during which he served as the party's presidential candidate three times and dominated the drafting of its platforms. Under his leadership, the Democrats moved away from Jackson's and Cleveland's commitment to minimal government and laissez-faire but they retained a Jacksonian distrust of monopoly and opposition to governmental favoritism toward business. Bryan and the other new leaders of the Democratic party accepted the Populists' conclusion that the solution to the problems of economic concentration lay not in the policies of laissez-faire but in using government to limit corporate power, especially monopoly power. "A private monopoly," Bryan never tired of repeating, "is indefensible and intolerable." His usual solution was to break up monopolies, but he sometimes advocated the Populist solution of government ownership.

Given the Democrats' perpetual minority status during the period of Bryan's party leadership, however, they could do little to translate these positions into policy. When the opportunity finally came, after 1912, it was under the leadership of Woodrow Wilson.

The Republicans, too, experienced a change in their leadership and their policy commitments. McKinley was the last of the Civil War generation to serve in the White House. Veterans of the Union armies had dominated Republican leadership for a generation, but that generation reached its end around 1900. When McKinley was assassinated in 1901, his passing, in effect, also marked the passing of a long-lived and highly influential generation of Republican leaders. As the last GAR members died or retired to the sidelines of politics, state and national nominating conventions turned to a new generation, to men like Theodore Roosevelt (born in 1858, and just six years old at the end of the Civil War), who became president upon the death of McKinley in 1901, or Robert La Follette (born in 1855), who won the governor's office in Wisconsin in 1900. Under Roosevelt's leadership, and with support from La Follette and others like him who were eventually to be called progressives, Republicans moved well beyond the hesitant steps of the Sherman Antitrust Act and the Erdman Act when, in 1906, they gave the Interstate Commerce Commission the power to set railroad rates—the real beginning of federal regulation of the economy. Their efforts, however, provoked a division within the Republican party, one that eventually led Roosevelt to break, briefly, with the Republicans and to seek the presidency as a Progressive in 1912.

After the mid-1890s, the majority of American voters considered themselves Republicans, but many voters in both parties held their new party commitments less intensely than they had in the Gilded Age. Before 1890, for most voters, ethnicity had closely coincided with their party affiliation. After the 1890s, more voters seem to have felt pulled toward one party by their economic situation and toward the other party by their ethnicity. Some voters became increasingly likely to vote a "split ticket," supporting Republicans for some offices and Democrats for others, something much easier to do because of the adoption of the Australian ballot. Other voters seem to have resolved such conflicts by not voting at all. As more and more government positions became subject to the merit system, there were fewer and fewer rewards for party workers who once had labored so strenuously to mobilize voters on election day. Southern black voters were not the only ones disfranchised by new laws. Voter registration laws and similar measures in the North disqualified significant numbers of other groups as well, especially migratory workers and recent immigrants. Voter participation began to decline: from 79 percent in 1896 to 65 percent in 1908 to 59 percent in 1912 (a year in which Republican voters were especially prone to cross-pressures) to 49 percent in 1920. The decline in party loyalties was both reflected in and accelerated by changes in election laws in some states that made some offices officially nonpartisan.

The political role of newspapers also changed. In the 1890s, technological advances in paper manufacturing and printing, together with increasing numbers of literate adults, encouraged the emergence of mass-circulation daily newspapers in major cities. Enterprising publishers, notably William Randolph Hearst and Joseph Pulitzer, transformed large urban newspapers through "yellow journalism," competing for the largest circulation through sensational headlines and stories. As they focused on increasing their circulation and advertising revenue, they had less need for subsidies from political parties. In fact, they sometimes saw a party commitment as an impediment to appealing to *all* potential readers. Thus, most of the new mass-circulation dailies played down their party ties. Some journalists also began to develop the idea of providing balanced coverage to both parties.

Parties, too, increasingly relied upon advertising. The 1896 campaign marked an acceleration of a shift already underway, from campaigning based on mobilizing voters and toward campaigning based on advertising the candidates. Some steps in that direction had occurred earlier, but the icy personality of Harrison and the stolidity of Cleveland had posed limits to such an approach. In 1896 and 1900, however, both parties sought to make the most of the attractive, even charismatic, personalities of their presidential (and, for the Republicans in 1900, vice-presidential) candidates.

The shift from mobilizing voters to advertising candidates was one part of the larger change in the nature of politics and parties that included the decline in voter turnout, the erosion of party loyalties and increase in ticket-splitting, the growth of the merit system in the civil service (thereby reducing both the patronage at parties' disposal and their ability to raise campaign funds by assessing their appointees), and changes in the party orientation of major newspapers. All these contributed to a decline in the power and influence of party organizations.

With the erosion of the importance of parties, politics came increasingly to reflect the interaction of organized interest groups. Such organizations sprouted in almost bewildering variety during the late nineteenth and early twentieth centuries. For many social and economic groups, organization had become indispensable. By revolutionizing travel and communication, the railroad, telegraph, and telephone had encouraged some Americans to think in regional or national terms and to form nationwide organizations that expressed their common concerns and promoted their common interests—including their political interests. Manufacturers, farmers, merchants, lawyers, and many others formed or revitalized organizations to advance their own interests, including the American Federation of Labor (formed in 1886), American Newspaper Publishers Association (1887), American Railway Association (1891), National Association of Manufacturers (1895), American Medical Association (reorganized in 1901), and the Farmers' Union (formed in 1902).

Such organizations to protect and advance particular interests were widespread, and many of these began to look to government for help. Merchants' associations and farmers' groups, for example, had long pushed for laws to regulate railroad freight rates, but many other voices now called for government action in a variety of other circumstances. Not all of the newly formed groups promoted the economic interests of their members—some had united to espouse ethnic, racial, gender, or disability issues, e.g., the Polish National Alliance (formed in 1880), National Association of the Deaf (1880), General Federation of Women's Clubs (1890), National Association of Colored Women (1896), and National German-American Alliance (1901). Others had benevolent objectives, including the American Red Cross Society (1881), Audubon Society (1886), National Consumers League (1899), and National Child Labor Committee (1904).

Organized in 1895, the Anti-Saloon League soon became the model for successful interest-group politics as it developed such a well-organized, single-minded force that it captured the support of most temperance advocates and established itself as the leading force opposed to alcohol. Proudly describing itself as "the Church in action against the saloon," it focused its antagonism against the saloon, attacking it as the least defensible element in the liquor industry. As League publications and activities made clear, they did not just oppose the saloon, but liquor itself. Unlike the Prohibition party, which had sought to distance its adherents from the older parties, the League endorsed any mainstream politicians who opposed "Demon Rum"—regardless of their party affiliation or stand on other issues. As the "dry" crusade demonstrated its growing political clout, increasing numbers of politicians lined up against the saloon.

During the 1890s, too, there emerged new models of urban politics. Unlike the Mugwumps, some urban reformers in the 1890s went beyond demands for honest and efficient governmental administration to address larger social and economic issues. Hazen Pingree, for example, a successful and socially prominent businessman, won election as mayor of Detroit in 1889. Initially an advocate of honest, efficient government, Pingree soon began to criticize the city's gas, electric, and streetcar companies for overcharging and providing poor service. The depression of 1893 led him to address the needs of the unemployed with measures that included work projects and community gardens. Another successful manufacturer, Samuel "Golden Rule" Jones, won election as mayor of Toledo, Ohio, in 1897. He boasted of conducting his factory on the Golden Rule—do unto others as you would have them to unto you—and brought the same ideal to city government. Jones led the way in introducing free public baths, free concerts in the public parks, free kindergartens (originally created as child-care centers for working mothers), and the eight-hour day for city employees.

James Phelan of San Francisco provides an example of a municipal reformer who advocated active involvement by city government in the city's economy. Son of a pioneer banker and equally at home in the worlds of politics, business, and the arts, Phelan attacked corruption in city government, won election as mayor in 1896, then led in adopting a new charter that strengthened the office of mayor and required citywide election of "supervisors" (the term used rather than "councilmen"). He argued that municipal ownership of public utilities was a necessity because regulation inevitably led to corruption, as the regulated companies tried to influence or control the government officials responsible for enforcing the regulations. Phelan secured a commitment to city ownership of public utilities in the new San Francisco charter that took effect in 1901.

During the 1890s, the cities also saw the emergence of new concepts of social welfare that eventually produced new public policies. Central to these developments was the settlement house, first developed at London's Toynbee Hall in 1884 and introduced to the United States after 1886. Some of the most famous settlement houses, including Hull House in Chicago and College Settlement in New York City, owed their existence to the enthusiasm of young female college graduates who staffed the settlements and raised funds from donors. Many others were sponsored by churches. Some developed ties to universities. Settlement houses provided assistance to poor families, especially the women and children of poor families, offering child care, instruction in better homemaking, English lessons for immigrants, and much more. The new institution spread rapidly, and more than one hundred settlement houses were in operation by 1900. Of the 3,000–4,000 settlement house workers active by the turn of the century, three-quarters of them were women and most were college-educated.

Settlement houses proved to be an important source of reform, and Hull House was especially prominent in this regard. Founded in 1889 by Jane Addams and Ellen Gates Starr, Hull House was the first settlement house in Chicago. Addams and other Hull House activists, especially Florence Kelley, challenged city politicians and lobbied state legislators, seeking cleaner streets, the abolition of child labor, health and safety regulations for factories, compulsory school attendance, and more. Such efforts brought national recognition. By the turn of the century, settlement house workers in many cities had begun to advocate new governmental policies at local and state levels and, eventually, at the national level. At the same time, they were also creating a new profession, social work, dominated by women. Several recent scholars have focused on the significance of gender in understanding this new approach to social welfare, and some have used the label "maternalist" to distinguish these new patterns from the male-oriented assistance typical of military pensions and from the varieties of social welfare then developing in Europe, which usually focused on the needs of male wage earners.

The beginnings of a social welfare policy marked one element in the slow emergence of a new concept of the state. The Pendleton Act had been slowly extended by each succeeding president, to the point where, by 1901, it covered more than two-fifths of all federal civilian employees—a bureaucracy tied not to party but instead to the state itself. State governments had experimented with regulating railroads and other public utilities, and the Sherman Antitrust Act and the Erdman Railway Labor Act both pointed to a federal role in the economy that went beyond distribution and moved in the direction of a regulatory state. The nation now had a real navy, and it had an insular empire to garrison and administer. Its new role in world affairs meant an increased role for the State Department, accelerating efforts to replace party hacks with more competent members of a professional diplomatic and consular service.

The organized interest groups that appeared so suddenly and in such numbers at the turn of the century grew out of many separate strands of social and economic development, often evolving over a quarter-century or more. From such disparate origins, many of these groups now looked to the political arena and to the emerging state. Business leaders now saw in the state a source of regulation—a prospect that some welcomed and promoted even as others tried to avoid the hand of federal regulation on their own endeavors. Some reformers hoped to restrain big business, and others were concerned about corruption in urban politics and the power of party bosses. Humanitarian groups raised concerns about victims of industrialization. Some middle- and upper-class Americans, frightened by labor strife and political unrest during the 1890s, hoped to use government to stabilize the social order. Some wanted to do so by suppressing unions, but others tried to address what they saw as the causes of social unrest—brutal poverty and irresponsible wealth. New health and social-service professionals, upon graduating from recently transformed universities, confidently sought to use the authority of the state to apply their technical knowledge and to shape a different future. Organized groups of women emerged onto the political scene as a major force, advocating a variety of social reforms and demanding their right to vote. Still other groups promoted other causes. Despite such diversity, most groups shared an optimism that responsible citizens, assisted by technical expertise and operating through government, could accelerate "progress"—the improvement of the human situation. As early as the 1890s, some of these reformers began calling themselves "progressive citizens."[2] Thus, the United States entered the new century and the Progressive Era.

---

2 The use of "progressive" as a noun, however, did not become widespread until somewhat later.

APPENDIX
Tables

Table 1.1	Farm Production and Crop Prices, 1865–1900

	Wheat		Corn		Cotton	
	Produc-tion	Price per	Produc-tion	Price per	Produc-tion	Price per
	Million	Bushel	*Million*	Bushel	*1,000*	pound
Year	*Bushels*	*Dollars*	*Bushels*	*Dollars*	*Bales*	*Cents*
1866	170	$2.06	731	$0.66	2,097	n.a.
1867	211	2.01	794	0.78	2,520	
1868	246	1.46	920	0.62	2,366	
1869	290	0.92	782	0.73	3,011	
1870	254	1.04	1,125	0.52	4,352	
1871	272	1.25	1,142	0.46	2,974	
1872	271	1.24	1,279	0.38	3,933	
1873	322	1.17	1,008	0.48	4,168	
1874	356	0.95	1,059	0.64	3,836	
1875	314	1.01	1,450	0.42	4,631	
1876	309	1.04	1,478	0.36	4,474	9.71¢
1877	396	1.08	1,516	0.36	4,773	8.53
1878	449	0.77	1,565	0.31	5,074	8.16
1879	459	1.11	1,752	0.36	5,756	10.28
1880	502	0.95	1,707	0.39	6,606	9.83
1881	406	1.20	1,245	0.63	5,456	10.66

cont'd

Table 1.1	Farm Production and Crop Prices, 1865–1900 cont'd

	Wheat		Corn		Cotton	
Year	Production Million Bushels	Price per Bushel Dollars	Production Million Bushels	Price per Bushel Dollars	Production 1,000 Bales	Price per pound Cents
1882	552	0.89	1,755	0.48	6,949	9.12
1883	439	0.91	1,652	0.42	5,713	9.13
1884	571	0.65	1,948	0.35	5,682	9.19
1885	400	0.77	2,058	0.32	6,576	8.39
1886	514	0.69	1,783	0.36	6,505	8.06
1887	491	0.68	1,605	0.43	6,047	8.55
1888	424	0.93	2,251	0.33	6,938	8.50
1889	504	0.70	2,294	0.28	7,473	8.55
1890	449	0.84	1,650	0.50	8,653	8.59
1891	678	0.83	2,336	0.40	9,035	7.24
1892	612	0.62	1,897	0.39	6,700	8.34
1893	506	0.53	1,900	0.36	7,493	7.00
1894	542	0.49	1,615	0.45	9,091	4.59
1895	542	0.51	2,535	0.25	7,162	7.62
1896	523	0.72	2,671	0.21	8,533	6.66
1897	606	0.81	2,288	0.26	10,899	6.68
1898	768	0.58	2,351	0.29	11,278	5.73
1899	655	0.59	2,646	0.30	9,346	6.98
1900	599	0.62	2,662	0.35	10.124	9.15

SOURCE: Adapted from Series K 503, 504, 507, 508, 554, 555, United States Department of Commerce, Bureau of the Census, *Historical Statistics of the United States: Colonial Times to 1970,* Bicentennial Edition, 2 parts (Washington: U.S. Government Printing Office, 1975), 1: 512, 518. Prices are average for December 1, rather than average paid at harvest.

Table 2.1 **Popular and Electoral Vote for President, 1868–1904**

Year	Popular vote				Electoral Vote		
	Demo-cratic	Repub-lican	Prohi-bition	Agrarian Parties*	Demo-cratic	Repub-lican	Agrarian Parties*
1868	46.7%	52.7%			80	214	
1872	43.9	55.6			66**	286	
1876	51.0	48.0		1.0%	184	185	
1880	48.0	48.5	0.1%	3.4	155	214	
1884	48.5	48.2	1.5	1.7	219	182	
1888	48.6	47.8	2.2	1.3	168	233	
1892	46.1	43.0	2.2	8.5	277	145	22
1896	46.7	51.0	0.9		176	271	
1900	45.5	51.7	1.5	0.4	155	292	
1904	37.6	56.4	1.9	0.9	140	336	

*Agrarian parties include:
    1876, Greenback;
    1880 and 1884, Greenback-Labor;
    1888, Union Labor;
    1892, People's (Populist); and
    1900, and 1904, Middle-of-the-Road Populist.

In 1896, the Populist party endorsed the Democratic candidate; one wing of the Populist party endorsed the Democratic candidate in 1900, and another wing, called the Middle-of-the-Road faction, ran its own candidate. Other parties receiving 1% or more of the popular vote include the National Democratic party (Gold Democrats) who received 1.0% in 1896 and the Socialist party with got 3.0% in 1904.

**Horace Greeley, the Democratic candidate, died before the members of the electoral college voted; this figure represents all electoral votes not cast for the Republican candidate.

SOURCE: Adapted from Series Y 80–83, United States Department of Commerce, Bureau of the Census, *Historical Statistics of the United States: Colonial Times to 1970,* Bicentennial Edition, 2 parts (Washington: U.S. Government Printing Office, 1975), 2: 1073.

Table 2.2	Electoral Votes by Selected Regions and States	
	1876, 1880	1884, 1888
Needed to Win:	185	201
Democratic States:		
Former Confederate		
States	95	98
Border States	43	46
New Jersey	9	9
Sub-total	147	153
"Swing" States:		
New York	35	36
Indiana	15	15
Connecticut	6	6
Total, these states:	203	210

SOURCE: Adapted from Series Y 84–134, United States Department of Commerce, Bureau of the Census, *Historical Statistics of the United States: Colonial Times to 1970,* Bicentennial Edition, 2 parts (Washington: U.S. Government Printing Office, 1975), 2: 1075–76.

Table 2.3 | Party Strength in Congress, 1868–1904

| | House of Representatives | | | | | Senate | | | | | Party winning or holding the presidency |
Year*	Democrats	Republicans	All Others	Maj. Party	Size of majority**	Democrats	Republicans	All Others	Maj. Party	Size of majority**	
1868	63	149		Rep	86	11	56		Rep	45	Republican
1870	104	134	5	Dem	30	17	52	5	Rep	35	Republican
1872	92	194	14	Rep	102	19	49	5	Rep	30	Republican
1874	169	109	14	Dem	60	29	45	2	Rep	16	Republican
1876	153	140		Dem	13	36	39	1	Rep	3	Republican
1878	149	130	14	Dem	19	42	33	1	Dem	9	Republican
1880	135	147	11	Rep	12	37	37	1	tie		Republican
1882	197	118	10	Dem	79	36	38	2	Rep	2	Republican
1884	183	140	2	Dem	43	34	43		Rep	9	Democrat
1886	169	152	4	Dem	17	37	39		Rep	2	Democrat
1888	159	166		Rep	7	37	39		Rep	2	Republican
1890	235	88	9	Dem	147	39	47	2	Rep	8	Republican
1892	218	127	11	Dem	91	44	38	3	Dem	6	Democrat
1894	105	244	7	Rep	139	39	43	6	Rep	4	Democrat
1896	113	204	40	Rep	91	34	47	7	Rep	13	Republican
1898	163	185	9	Rep	22	26	53	8	Rep	27	Republican
1900	151	197	9	Rep	46	31	55	4	Rep	24	Republican
1902	178	208		Rep	30	33	57		Rep	24	Republican
1904	136	250		Rep	114	33	57		Rep	24	Republican

*The year when the House members were elected; the Congress in which they served met during the two years following. Thus, the Congress elected in 1878 met for its first session in December 1879 and continued in session into 1881.

**The size of majority is simply the difference between the two major parties, and does not take into account that members of minor parties sometimes worked out long-term alignments with one of the major parties for the purposes of organizing each house, securing committee assignments, and, sometimes, voting and influencing patronage.

SOURCE: Adapted from Series Y 204-210, United States Department of Commerce, Bureau of the Census, *Historical Statistics of the United States: Colonial Times to 1970,* Bicentennial Edition, 2 parts (Washington: U.S. Government Printing Office, 1975), 2: 1083.

Table 2.4	Federal Income and Expenses, including Customs Receipts

Year	Total Federal Receipts	Total Federal Expenditures	Federal Surplus or Deficit	Federal Receipts from Customs	Ratio of Customs Duties to Total Value of Imports
	------------------*All in thousands of dollars*------------------				
1866	558,033	520,809	37,223	179,047	41.81
1867	490,634	357,543	133,091	176,418	44.56
1868	405,634	377,340	28,298	164,465	46.56
1869	370,944	322,865	48,078	180,048	44.76
1870	411,255	309,654	101,602	194,538	44.89
- *Tariff of 1870* -					
1871	383,324	292,177	91,147	206,270	40.51
1872	374,107	277,518	96,589	216,370	37.99
- *Tariff of 1872* -					
1873	333,738	290,345	43,393	188,090	27.90
1874	304,979	302,634	2,345	163,014	28.29
1875	288,000	274,623	13,377	157,168	29.36
1876	294,096	265,101	28,995	148,072	31.25
1877	281,406	241,334	40,072	130,956	29.20
1878	257,764	236,964	20,800	130,171	29.00
1879	273,827	266,948	6,879	137,250	30.33
1880	333,527	267,643	65,884	186,522	29.12
1881	360,782	260,713	100,069	198,160	29.79
1882	403,525	257,981	145,544	220,411	30.16
1883	398,288	265,408	132,879	214,706	30.04
- - - - - - - - - - - - - - - - - - - *"Mongrel Tariff"* -					
1884	348,520	244,126	104,394	195,067	28.50
1885	323,691	260,227	63,464	217,287	30.75
1886	336,440	242,483	93,957	192,905	30.35
1887	371,403	267,932	103,471	217,287	31.52
1888	379,266	267,925	111,341	219,091	30.55
1889	387,050	299,289	87,761	223,833	30.02
1890	403,081	318,041	85,040	229,669	29.59

cont'd

Table 2.4	**Federal Income and Expenses, including Customs Receipts cont'd**				
Year	Total Federal Receipts	Total Federal Expenditures	Federal Surplus or Deficit	Federal Receipts from Customs	Ratio of Customs Duties to Total Value of Imports
	------------------*All in thousands of dollars*------------------				Imports
			McKinley Tariff		
1891	392,612	365,774	26,839	219,522	25.65
1892	354,938	345,023	9,914	177,453	21.65
1893	385,820	383,478	2,342	203,355	23.91
1894	306,355	367,525	-61,170	131,819	20.56
			Wilson-Gorman Tariff		
1895	324,729	356,195	-31,466	152,159	20.44
1896	338,142	352,179	-14,037	160,022	20.67
1897	347,722	365,774	-18,052	176,554	21.89
			Dingley Tariff		
1898	405,321	443,369	-38,047	149,575	24.77
1899	515,961	605,072	-89,112	206,128	29.48
1900	567,241	520,861	46,380	233,165	27.62

SOURCE: Adapted from Series Y 335, 336,337, 353, United States Department of Commerce, Bureau of the Census, *Historical Statistics of the United States: Colonial Times to 1970,* Bicentennial Edition, 2 parts (Washington: U.S. Government Printing Office, 1975), 2: 1104, 1106.

BIBLIOGRAPHICAL ESSAY

This bibliographical essay is intended both to identify the major works from which this book has been drawn and to suggest additional readings for those further interested in particular aspects of Gilded Age politics. Vincent P. DeSantis has compiled a very useful bibliography, *The Gilded Age, 1877–1896* (1973), that includes most significant works, primary and secondary, up to the time of its publication.

General Overviews

The two most important syntheses of Gilded Age politics to appear in the past few decades are H. Wayne Morgan, *From Hayes to McKinley: National Party Politics, 1877–1896* (1969), and Morton Keller, *Affairs of State: Public Life in Late Nineteenth Century America* (1977); they both deserve a careful reading from the serious student of the politics of this period. Morgan includes an extensive bibliography; Keller has none. In addition, there are the eight volumes of James Ford Rhodes's *History of the United States from the Compromise of 1850 to the McKinley-Bryan Campaign of 1896* (1920) and his *The McKinley and Roosevelt Administrations* (1922), works most useful, perhaps, as references. For a less extensive but recent and analytical overview of the period, see Richard L. McCormick, "Public Life in Industrial America, 1877–

1917," in *The New American History*, ed. Eric Foner (1990). General treatments of the Gilded Age that have appeared since the 1960s and that provide significant coverage of politics include John A. Garraty, *The New Commonwealth, 1877–1890* (1968); Carl Degler, *The Age of the Economic Revolution, 1876–1900*, 2nd ed. (1977); Nell Irvin Painter, *Standing at Armageddon: The United States, 1877–1919* (1987); and Vincent P. DeSantis, *The Shaping of Modern America, 1877–1920*, 2nd ed. (1989). Robert H. Wiebe, *The Search for Order, 1877–1920* (1967), while interesting in many ways, provides little coverage of Gilded Age politics.

There are a great many memoirs, autobiographies, and biographies of the period's prominent political figures. DeSantis's bibliography lists more than two hundred autobiographies or biographies as of 1973, including works on nearly all significant figures and many of less prominence, and the number of biographies has grown considerably since then.

Chapter One

During the 1960s and 1970s, historians developed new understandings of the parties and politics of the late nineteenth century, prompted initially by the work of political scientists in analyzing voting behavior. The work of V. O. Key, Jr., and research on contemporary politics conducted at the University of Michigan's Survey Research Center in the 1950s and 1960s contributed to a reconceptualization of politics that often went under the label "behavioralism." Lee Benson sounded the call for a new political history in 1957, in "Research Problems in American Political Historiography," in *Common Frontiers of the Social Sciences*, ed. Mirra Komarovsky (1957). The essays of Samuel P. Hays that helped to define the "new political history" are collected in *American Political History as Social History* (1980). Among the monographs that developed the new political history for the Gilded Age are Frederick C. Luebke, *Immigrants and Politics: The Germans of Nebraska, 1880–1900* (1969); Richard Jensen, *The Winning of the Midwest: Social and Political Conflict, 1888–1896* (1971); Samuel T. McSeveney, *The Politics of Depression: Political Be-*

havior in the Northeast, 1893–1896 (1972); J. Morgan Kousser, *The Shaping of Southern Politics: Suffrage Restriction and the Establishment of the One-Party South, 1880–1910* (1974); and Melvyn Hammarberg, *The Indiana Voter: The Historical Dynamics of Party Allegiance during the 1870's* (1977). Paul Kleppner's work is especially important as well as being the most extensive: *The Cross of Culture: A Social Analysis of Midwestern Politics, 1850–1900* (1970), *The Third Electoral System, 1853–1892: Voters, Parties, and Political Cultures* (1979), *The Evolution of American Electoral Systems* (1981), *Who Voted? The Dynamics of Electoral Turnout, 1870–1980* (1982), and *Continuity and Change in Electoral Politics, 1893–1928* (1987). Other important perspectives are to be found in Robert Kelley's *The Cultural Pattern in American Politics: The First Century* (1979) and Jean H. Baker's *Affairs of Party: The Political Culture of Northern Democrats in the Mid-Nineteenth Century* (1983). For a historiographical perspective on one crucial aspect of the "new political history," see Ronald P. Formisano, "The Invention of the Ethnocultural Interpretation," *American Historical Review* 99 (1994): 453–477. Three recent works also deserve special attention: Michael McGerr, *The Decline of Popular Politics: The American North, 1865–1928* (1986); Richard L. McCormick, *The Party Period and Public Policy: American Politics from the Age of Jackson to the Progressive Era* (1986); and Peter H. Argersinger, *Structure, Process, and Party: Essays in American Political History* (1992).

On parties, elections, and patronage in the late nineteenth century, start with the accounts of two contemporary observers from abroad: James Bryce, *The American Commonwealth* (1888), and Moisei Ostrogorski, *Democracy and the Organization of Political Parties*, vol. 2, *The United States* (1902). The many autobiographies and biographies of political figures also provide a great deal of anecdotal information on parties, elections, and patronage. Other useful sources on parties and patronage include Leonard D. White, *The Republican Era: A Study in Administrative History, 1869–1901* (1958); Ari Hoogenboom, *Outlawing the Spoils: A History of the Civil Service Reform Movement, 1865–1883* (1961); Robert D. Marcus, *Grand Old Party: Political Structure in the Gilded Age, 1880–1896* (1971); and Theda Skocpol, *Protecting*

Soldiers and Mothers: The Political Origins of Social Policy in the United States (1992). The subject of party finance is treated in Clifton K. Yearley, *The Money Machines: The Breakdown and Reform of Governmental and Party Finance in the North, 1860–1920* (1970.) For statistical analyses of party loyalty, see William Claggett and John Van Wingen, "The 'Onward March of Party Decomposition' in the American Electorate," *Social Science History* 17 (1993): 37–70, and Kleppner, *Continuity and Change*. See also Peter H. Argersinger, "New Perspectives on Election Fraud in the Gilded Age," *Political Science Quarterly* 100 (winter 1985–86): 669–687; and Walter Dean Burnham, "Those High Nineteenth-Century American Voting Turnouts: Fact or Fiction?" *Journal of Interdisciplinary History* 16 (1986): 613–644.

Many historians have been attracted to the study of the party bosses of the period, especially the city bosses. The most important works on city bosses appear in the bibliography in Raymond A. Mohl, *The New City: Urban America in the Industrial Age, 1860–1920* (1985); for an evaluation of such works, see Jon C. Teaford, "Finis for Tweed and Steffens: Rewriting the History of Urban Rule," *Reviews in American History* 10 (1982): 133–149. Among urban politicians of the era, George Washington Plunkitt stands out for the extent to which his observations (first published in 1905) have been taken to epitomize the species; Terrence J. McDonald provides a particularly good introduction to a recent edition: *Plunkitt of Tammany Hall*, ed. Terrence J. McDonald (1994). For sharply contrasting views of the Tweed Ring, see Seymour J. Mandelbaum, *Boss Tweed's New York* (1965); Alexander B. Callow, Jr., *The Tweed Ring* (1966); and Leo Hershkowitz, *Tweed's New York: Another Look* (1977). For Nast's treatment of Tweed and his political contributions more generally, see Morton Keller, *The Art and Politics of Thomas Nast* (1968). For leading state bosses, see David M. Jordan, *Roscoe Conkling of New York: Voice in the Senate* (1971); James A. Kehl, *Boss Rule in the Gilded Age: Matt Quay of Pennsylvania* (1981); and James P. Jones, *John A. Logan: Stalwart Republican from Illinois* (1982).

For the Republicans and Democrats, in addition to the general histories of the period and the autobiographies and biographies of party leaders, see the national party platforms, which have been conveniently presented in Donald Bruce Johnson and Kirk H. Porter, *National Party Platforms*, various editions (1956 and later years). For the Republicans, see Vincent P. DeSantis, "The Republican Party Revisited, 1877–1897," in *The Gilded Age: A Reappraisal*, ed. H. Wayne Morgan (1963); Allan Peskin, "Who Were the Stalwarts? Who Were Their Rivals? Republican Factions in the Gilded Age," *Political Science Quarterly* 99 (1984–85): 703–716; Robert S. Salisbury, "The Republican Party and Positive Government: 1860–1890," *Mid-America* 68 (1986): 15–32; and William E. Gienapp, *The Origins of the Republican Party, 1852–1856* (1987). For Republican efforts to build a southern wing to their party, see Vincent P. DeSantis, *Republicans Face the Southern Question: The New Departure Years, 1877–1897* (1959); Stanley P. Hirshson, *Farewell to the Bloody Shirt: Northern Republicans and the Southern Negro, 1877–1893* (1962); Numan V. Bartley, "In Search of the New South: Southern Politics after Reconstruction," *Reviews in American History* 10 (1982): 150–163; and Richard H. Abbott, *The Republican Party and the South, 1855–1877: The First Southern Strategy* (1986).

For African Americans and politics, see Bess Beatty, *A Revolution Gone Backward: The Black Response to National Politics, 1876–1896* (1987); Lawanda Cox, "From Emancipation to Segregation: National Policy and Southern Blacks," in John Boles and Evelyn Thomas Nolen, eds., *Interpreting Southern History* (1987); and William S. McFeely, *Frederick Douglass* (1991).

For Democrats, see Alexander C. Flick, *Samuel Jones Tilden: A Study in Political Sagacity* (1939); Horace S. Merrill, *Bourbon Democracy of the Middle West, 1865–1896* (1953); Robert Kelley's treatment of Tilden in his *The Transatlantic Persuasion: The Liberal-Democratic Mind in the Age of Gladstone* (1969); R. Hal Williams, "'Dry Bones and Dead Language': The Democratic Party," in *The Gilded Age*, rev. ed., H. Wayne Morgan, ed.,(1970); R. Hal Williams, *The Democratic Party and California Politics, 1880–1896* (1973); Lawrence Grossman, *The Democratic Party and the Negro: Northern and National Politics, 1868–92* (1976); Jerome Mushkat, *The Reconstruction of the New York Democracy, 1861–1874* (1981); and Kelley, "The Democracy of Tilden and Cleveland," in *Democrats and the American Idea*, ed. Peter B.

Kovler (1992). For the American Protective Association, see Donald Louis Kinzer, *An Episode in Anti-Catholicism: The American Protective Association* (1964).

The Mugwumps are treated, among other places, in Richard Hofstadter, *The American Political Tradition* (1948); John G. Sproat, *"The Best Men": Liberal Reformers in the Gilded Age* (1968, 1982); and John M. Dobson, *Politics in the Gilded Age: A New Perspective on Reform* (1972).

There is a large quantity of literature on women and politics in the Gilded Age. For perceptive overviews, see Suzanne Lebsock, "Women and American Politics, 1880–1920," in *Women, Politics, and Change*, ed. Louise A. Tilly and P. Gurin (1990); and Paula Baker, "The Domestication of Politics: Women and American Political Society, 1780–1920," *American Historical Review* 89 (1984): 620–647. For the suffrage movement, see Elizabeth Cady Stanton, Susan B. Anthony, and Matilda Joslyn Gage, eds., *History of Woman Suffrage* (1881–1922); Aileen S. Kraditor, *The Ideas of the Woman Suffrage Movement, 1890–1920* (1965); Eleanor Flexner, *Century of Struggle: The Woman's Rights Movement in the United States*, rev. ed. (1975); Elisabeth Griffith, *In Her Own Right: The Life of Elizabeth Cady Stanton* (1984); Beverly Beeton, *Women Vote in the West: The Woman Suffrage Movement, 1869–1896* (1986); and Kathleen Barry, *Susan B. Anthony* (1988).

For the prohibitionists, many of whom were women, see Jack S. Blocker, Jr., *Retreat from Reform: The Prohibition Movement in the United States, 1890–1913* (1976); Ruth Bordin, *Woman and Temperance: The Quest for Power and Liberty, 1873–1900* (1981); Barbara L. Epstein, *The Politics of Domesticity: Women, Evangelism, and Temperance in Nineteenth-century America* (1981); Ruth Bordin, *Frances Willard* (1986); and Richard F. Hamm, *Shaping the Eighteenth Amendment: Temperance Reform, Legal Culture, and the Polity, 1880–1920* (1995).

The grangers are treated in Solon J. Buck, *The Granger Movement: A Study of Agricultural Organization and Its Political, Economic and Social Manifestation, 1870–1880* (1913); Thomas A. Woods, *Knights of the Plow: Oliver H. Kelley and the Origins of the Grange in Republican Ideology* (1991); and Donald B. Marti,

Women of the Grange: Mutuality and Sisterhood in Rural America, 1866–1920 (1991). On the so-called granger laws, see Lee Benson, *Merchants, Farmers, and Railroads: Railroad Regulation and New York Politics, 1850–1887* (1955); Gabriel Kolko, *Railroads and Regulation, 1877–1916* (1965); George H. Miller, *Railroads and the Granger Laws* (1971); and Ari and Olive Hoogenboom, *A History of the ICC: From Panacea to Palliative* (1976).

On greenbackers, silverites, and monetary policy issues more generally, see Milton Friedman and Anna Jacobson Schwartz, *A Monetary History of the United States, 1867–1960* (1963); Irwin Unger, *The Greenback Era: A Social and Political History of American Finance, 1865–1879* (1964); Walter T. K. Nugent, *The Money Question during Reconstruction* (1967); Nugent, *Money and American Society, 1865–1880* (1968); and Allen Weinstein, *Prelude to Populism: Origins of the Silver Issue, 1867–1878* (1970). The latter four works are also important for currency policy issues during the Grant and Hayes administrations.

On labor and labor parties, see especially Richard Ostreicher, "Urban Working-Class Political Behavior and Theories of American Electoral Politics," *Journal of American History* 74 (1988): 1257–1286; and Leon Fink, *Workingmen's Democracy: The Knights of Labor and American Politics* (1983). See also Charles Albro Barker, *Henry George* (1955); David Montgomery, *Beyond Equality: Labor and the Radical Republicans, 1862–1872* (1967); Alexander Saxton, *The Indispensable Enemy: Labor and the Anti-Chinese Movement in California* (1971); Vincent J. Falzone, *Terence V. Powderly, Middle Class Reformer* (1978); Susan Levine, *Labor's True Woman: Carpet Weavers, Industrialization, and Labor Reform in the Gilded Age* (1984); Gwendolyn Mink, *Old Labor and New Immigrants in American Political Development: Union, Party, and State, 1875–1920* (1986); Neil L. Shumsky, *The Evolution of Political Protest and the Workingmen's Party of California* (1991); and David Montgomery, *Citizen Worker: The Experience of Workers in the United States with Democracy and the Free Market during the Nineteenth Century* (1993).

Despite its importance, there has been relatively little done on the history of the secret ballot. The only recent work is Lionel E. Fredman, *The Australian Ballot* (1968).

On parties and the state, see the work of some of the leading figures in the "new institutionalism": Stephen Skowronek, *Building a New American State: The Expansion of National Administrative Capacities, 1877–1920* (1982); Richard F. Bensel, *Yankee Leviathan: The Origins of Central State Authority in America, 1859–1877* (1990); and Skocpol, *Protecting Soldiers and Mothers*. For an overview of the "new institutionalism," see David B. Robertson, "The Return to History and the New Institutionalism in America," *Social Science History* 17 (1993): 1–36. Hamm, in *Shaping the Eighteenth Amendment*, disputes some of the new institutionalists' assumptions but acknowledges the importance of their concerns; he argues for use of "polity" rather than "state."

An important dimension is provided by Ballard C. Campbell, *Representative Democracy: Public Policy and Midwestern Legislatures in the Late Nineteenth Century* (1980), which emphasizes the active nature of state government; Campbell has also argued that study of state governments provides evidence that contradicts Skowronek's argument that the nineteenth-century state consisted solely of "parties and courts."

Chapter Two

In addition to the treatments of national politics already noted, see David J. Rothman, *Politics and Power: The United States Senate, 1869–1901* (1966). On the tariff, see Edward Stanwood, *American Tariff Controversies in the Nineteenth Century* (1903); Frank W. Taussig, *The Tariff History of the United States*, 8th ed. (1931); Tom E. Terrill, *The Tariff, Politics, and American Foreign Policy, 1874–1901* (1973); G. R. Hawke, "The United States Tariff and Industrial Protection in the Late Nineteenth Century," *Economic History Review* 28 (1975): 84–99; Joseph F. Kenkel, *Progressives and Protection: The Search for a Tariff Policy, 1866–1936* (1983); and Judith Goldstein, *Ideas, Interests, and American Trade Policy* (1993).

The most thorough account of Grant's troubled presidency remains William B. Hesseltine, *Ulysses S. Grant: Politician* (1935, 1957, 1967); but see also William S. McFeely, *Grant: A Biography* (1981) and John A. Carpenter, *Ulysses S. Grant* (1970). For major policy issues of the Grant years, see Eric Foner, *Reconstruction: America's Unfinished Revolution, 1863–1877* (1988); William Gillette, *Retreat from Reconstruction: 1869–1879* (1979); Margaret S. Thompson, *The "Spider Web": Congress and Lobbying in the Age of Grant* (1985); William H. Hale, *Horace Greeley: Voice of the People* (1950); Erik S. Lunde, *Horace Greeley* (1981); Allan Nevins, *Hamilton Fish: The Inner History of the Grant Administration*, 2 vols., rev. ed. (1957). For an overview of Grant's "peace policy," as well as later developments in Indian policy, and a good bibliography of related works, see Philip Weeks, *Farewell, My Nation: The American Indian and the United States, 1820–1890* (1990).

For the election of 1876 and the Compromise of 1877, the classic study is C. Vann Woodward's *Reunion and Reaction: The Compromise of 1877 and the End of Reconstruction*, rev. ed. (1956). For a more recent treatment, see Keith I. Polakoff, *The Politics of Inertia: The Election of 1876 and the End of Reconstruction* (1973).

For Rutherford B. Hayes, see Ari Hoogenboom, *Rutherford B. Hayes: Warrior and President* (1995), and Hoogenboom, *The Presidency of Rutherford B. Hayes* (1988). For major policy issues of the Hayes administration, see the works already noted on the Republican party and the South; Robert V. Bruce, *1877: Year of Violence* (1959); and the works already noted on currency policy. See also Emily Geer, *First Lady: The Life of Lucy Webb Hayes* (1984).

For the Garfield and Arthur administrations, see Allan Peskin, *Garfield: A Biography* (1978); George F. Howe, *Chester A. Arthur: A Quarter-century of Machine Politics* (1934); Thomas C. Reeves, *Gentleman Boss: The Life of Chester Alan Arthur* (1975); and, especially, Justus D. Doenecke, *The Presidencies of James A. Garfield and Chester A. Arthur* (1981). For major issues and policies, see S. Walter Poulshock, *The Two Parties and the Tariff in the 1880's* (1965); Saxton, *Indispensable Enemy*; Elmer C. Sand-meyer, *The Anti-Chinese Movement in California*, foreword by Roger Daniels (1939, 1973); Jordan, *Conkling*; and Hoogenboom, *Outlawing the Spoils*.

The most recent, and most judicious, treatment of Cleveland's presidency is Richard E. Welch, Jr., *The Presidencies of Grover Cleveland* (1988). Older, highly laudatory biographies include Allan Nevins, *Grover Cleveland: A Study in Courage* (1933, 1966), and Robert McElroy, *Grover Cleveland: The Man and the Statesman*, 2 vols. (1923); much more critical is Horace S. Merrill, *Bourbon Leader: Grover Cleveland and the Democratic Party* (1957). See also John F. Marszalek, *Grover Cleveland: A Bibliography* (1988). For major policy issues, see Hoogenboom and Hoogenboom, *History of the ICC*; Delos S. Otis, *The Dawes Act and the Allotment of Indian Lands* (1934, 1973); Henry E. Fritz, *The Movement for Indian Assimilation, 1860–1890* (1963, 1981); Frederick E. Hoxie, "The End of the Savage: Indian Policy in the United States Senate, 1880–1900," *Chronicles of Oklahoma* 55 (1977): 157–179; Hoxie, *A Final Promise: The Campaign to Assimilate the Indians, 1880–1920* (1984); Abraham Blinderman, "Congressional Social Darwinism and the American Indian," *Indian Historian* 11 (1978): 15–17; the various tariff histories; Joanne Reitano, *The Tariff Question in the Gilded Age: The Great Debate of 1888* (1994); and James L. Baumgardner, "The 1888 Presidential Election: How Corrupt?" *Presidential Studies Quarterly* 14 (1984): 416–427.

For Harrison and the Fifty-first Congress, see Morgan, *From Hayes to McKinley*; Homer E. Socolofsky and Allan B. Spetter, *The Presidency of Benjamin Harrison* (1987); R. Hal Williams, *Years of Decision: American Politics in the 1890s* (1978); and Harry J. Sievers, *Benjamin Harrison*, vols. 2–3 (1952–1960). For major policy issues, see B. Franklin Cooling, *Benjamin Franklin Tracy: Father of the Modern American Fighting Navy* (1973); Skocpol, *Protecting Soldiers and Mothers*; John A. Garraty, *Henry Cabot Lodge, A Biography* (1953); William Letwin, *Law and Economic Policy in America: The Evolution of the Sherman Antitrust Act* (1965, 1981); and the tariff and currency histories.

Chapter Three

For party systems and critical realignments, see Walter Dean Burnham, *Critical Elections and the Mainsprings of American Politics* (1970); William N. Chambers and Burnham, eds., *The American Party Systems: Stages of Political Development*, rev. ed. (1975); Jerome M. Clubb, William H. Flanigan, and Nancy H. Zingale, eds., *Partisan Realignment: Voters, Parties, and Government in American History* (1980, 1990); William Claggett, ed., "Walter Dean Burnham and the Dynamics of American Politics" (special issue) *Social Science History* 10 (1986): 205–314; and David W. Brady, *Critical Elections and Congressional Policy Making* (1988).

The historiography of Populism is a long and at times bitter one. For a quarter of a century after the appearance of Richard Hofstadter's *The Age of Reform from Bryan to F.D.R.* (1955), studies of Populism mirrored scholarly disputes over the interpretation of American history more generally. A full survey of this closely contested historiographic terrain could fill a book by itself. Recent summaries of the historiography include Martin Ridge, "Populism Redux: John D. Hicks and *The Populist Revolt*," *Reviews in American History* 13 (1985): 142–54, and William F. Holmes, "Populism: In Search of Context," *Agricultural History* 64 (1990): 26–58. Two concise syntheses of Populism have also appeared recently: Gene Clanton, *Populism: The Humane Preference in America* (1991), and Robert C. McMath, *American Populism: A Social History, 1877–1898* (1993). See also the recent anthology edited by William F. Holmes, *American Populism* (1994). For more complete listings of the major works on Populism, consult the extensive bibliographies in all three of these works. Important works too recent to be in those bibliographies include Jeffrey Ostler, *Prairie Populism: The Fate of Agrarian Radicalism in Kansas, Nebraska, and Iowa, 1880–1892* (1993); Peter H. Argersinger, *The Limits of Agrarian Radicalism: Western Populism and American Politics* (1995); and Michael Kazin, *The Populist Persuasion: An American History* (1995). The account of Populism presented here draws upon primary sources and many of the studies by historians, but two older works deserve special mention: John D. Hicks, *The Populist Revolt: A History of the Farmers' Alliance and the People's Party* (1931, 1961); and Chester McArthur Destler, *American Radicalism, 1865–1901* (1946, 1963). This account does not accept the distinction between "movement culture" Populism and a "shadow movement" Populism drawn by Lawrence Goodwyn in *Democratic Promise: The Populist Moment in America* (1976).

For the 1892 election, see George H. Knoles, *The Presidential Campaign and Election of 1892* (1942). For Cleveland's second administration, see Welch, *The Presidencies of Grover Cleveland*; the Cleveland biographies; the tariff histories; Williams, *Years of Decision*; and J. Rogers Hollingsworth, *The Whirligig of Politics: The Democracy of Cleveland and Bryan* (1963). For specific policy issues, see Carlos Schwantes, *Coxey's Army: An American Odyssey* (1985); Almont Lindsey, *The Pullman Strike: The Story of a Unique Experiment and of a Great Labor Upheaval* (1942, 1977); and Nick Salvatore, *Eugene V. Debs: Citizen and Socialist* (1982).

On the election of 1896, see Stanley L. Jones, *The Presidential Election of 1896* (1964) and Paul W. Glad, *McKinley, Bryan, and the People* (1964). Several works on political behavior already cited focused centrally on the realignment of the 1890s, including Brady, *Critical Elections and Congressional Policy Making*; Burnham, *Critical Elections and the Mainsprings;* Jensen, *Winning of the Midwest*; Kleppner, *Cross of Culture;* Luebke, *Immigrants and Politics*; and McSeveney, *Politics of Depression*. For Bryan, see Paul W. Glad, *The Trumpet Soundeth: William Jennings Bryan and his Democracy* (1960); Paolo E. Coletta, *William Jennings Bryan*, 3 vols. (1964–69); Louis W. Koenig, *Bryan: A Political Biography* (1971); Robert W. Cherny, *A Righteous Cause: The Life of William Jennings Bryan* (1985, 1994); LeRoy Ashby, *William Jennings Bryan: Champion of Democracy* (1987).

For McKinley and his administration, see H. Wayne Morgan, *William McKinley and his America* (1963); Lewis L. Gould, "William McKinley and the Expansion of Presidential Power," *Ohio History* 87 (1978): 5–20; Gould, *The Presidency of William*

McKinley (1980); Joel Budgor et al., "The 1896 Election and Congressional Modernization," *Social Science History* 5 (1981): 53–90; and Lewis L. Gould and Craig H. Roell, *William McKinley: A Bibliography* (1988).

For a sampling of works that deal with the important changes in politics and policies during and immediately after the mid-1890s, see Brady, *Critical Elections and Congressional Policy Making*; Robert W. Cherny, "The Democratic Party in the Era of William Jennings Bryan," and John Milton Cooper, Jr., "Wilsonian Democracy," in *Democrats and the American Idea*, ed. Peter Kovler (1992); Melvyn Dubofsky, *The State and Labor in Modern America* (1994); Robert L. Beisner, *From the Old Diplomacy to the New, 1865–1900*, 2nd ed. (1986); Allen F. Davis, *Spearheads for Reform: The Social Settlements and the Progressive Movement, 1890–1914* (1967); Kathryn Kish Sklar, *Florence Kelley and the Nation's Work*, vol. 1, *The Rise of Women's Political Culture, 1830–1900* (1995); Nancy F. Cott, *The Grounding of Modern Feminism* (1987); K. Austin Kerr, *Organized for Prohibition: A New History of the Anti-Saloon League* (1985); Daniel T. Rodgers, "In Search of Progressivism," *Reviews in American History* 10 (1982): 113–132; Arthur S. Link and Richard L. McCormick, *Progressivism* (1983); Samuel P. Hays, *Conservation and the Gospel of Efficiency: The Progressive Conservation Movement, 1890–1920* (1959); Melvin G. Holli, *Reform in Detroit: Hazen S. Pingree and Urban Politics* (1969); Philip J. Ethington, *The Public City: The Political Construction of Urban Life in San Francisco, 1850–1900* (1994); David P. Thelen, *The New Citizenship: Origins of Progressivism in Wisconsin, 1885–1900* (1972); Richard L. McCormick, *From Realignment to Reform: Political Change in New York State, 1893–1910* (1979); Richard L. Watson, Jr., "From Populism Through the New Deal: Southern Political History," in John B. Boles and Evelyn Thomas Nolen, eds., *Interpreting Southern History* (1987); Dewey W. Grantham, *The Life and Death of the Solid South: A Political History* (1988); William A. Link, *The Paradox of Southern Progressivism, 1880–1930* (1992).

INDEX

American Politics in the Gilded Age, 1868–1900

Developmental editor and copy editor: Andrew J. Davidson
Proofreader: Claudia Siler
Production Editor: Lucy Herz
Typesetters: Linda Gaio Davidson, Lucy Herz, and Bruce Leckie
Cartographer: Kristin Bergstrom
Printer: McNaughton & Gunn, Inc.